The Enders M. Vorhees, *U.S. Steel ore carrier, is escorted into the icy waters of Lake Superior.*

Lake Carriers

The saga of the
Great Lakes fleet —
North America's
fresh water merchant marine

by JACQUES LESSTRANG
author of Seaway

A SALISBURY PRESS BOOK
A division of Superior Publishing Company
Seattle, Washington

Library of Congress Cataloging in Publication Data

LesStrang, Jacques.
Lake Carriers.

"A Salisbury Press book."
Includes index.

1. Shipping — Great Lakes — History.   I. Title.
HE630.G7L47   386'.5'0977   77-3052
ISBN 0-87564-217-9

FIRST EDITION

Printed and Bound in Canada by Evergreen Press, Ltd.,
Vancouver, B.C.

This book is for my mother,
Ada Marie LesStrang
whose quiet, yet consistent courage set
a standard for her generation, and for mine.

Introduction

The Lake Carriers rounds out a major work on the Great Lakes, the first volume of which, *Seaway,* was published last year.

Aside from being part of this greater whole, *The Lake Carriers* has a special meaning to me, both as an author and as a maritime publisher myself. I have wanted to write this book for a very long time. Not because I consider myself a historian, or even a ship fancier. But because it needed to be done. The saga of the lake carrier today — the Great Lakes fleet — is an epic story, unlike any other maritime adventure. And this heroic story had to be told, I felt, not only from the perspective of the past, which has already been done by others, but rather from that of the present.

I have divided this volume into two sections, primarily to separate the past — as colorful, as romantic and as inexplicable a part of the total story as it may be — from today's fleet and today's adventure.

There is some overlap, to be sure, and I am sorry for this; but there is no real way to draw a demarcation. Or I am not smart enough to do it.

A lot of people helped me with this book: USCG Vice Admiral (Ret.) Paul Trimble, who heads the Lake Carriers' Association and his Canadian counterpart, Rear Admiral (Ret.) Robert W. Timbrell of the Dominion Marine Association. David Van Brunt at U.S. Steel. The Lake Carriers' John Packard. And Howard Weiss, who provided such fine color photography deserves a very special mention. Special thanks go to John Seefeldt at Milwaukee; Tom Burke formerly Duluth; The Pittsburgh-Conneaut Dock Co., The Niagara Frontier Transportation Authority, Port of Chicago and finally, John Jursa at Toronto for their help in locating historic photographs for the book.

And every writer should have the assistance of a person like Michelle Cortright, whose research and editorial assistance added immeasurably to the effort. Whatever long-term value this volume might have is due in no small measure to her efforts. And, of course, I must thank my wife Barbara, who is always there, and who always understands.

J.L.

Oracabessa, Jamaica, W.I. and
Harbor Island, Glen Lake, Michigan

Contents

A close fit.

1

The Beginnings of Commerce

Perhaps nowhere in the world is there so unique a merchant marine as the several hundred vessels which comprise the Great Lakes fleet of the United States and Canada.

Within the shores of these five inland seas and along the reaches of the mighty St. Lawrence River exist a maritime commerce that equals or exceeds that of most of the nations of the world.

Here, the vessels of two nations ply fresh waters as expansive and often more angry than many of the salt water seas of the world, carrying cargoes of ores and fossil fuels and grains to the deep-draft ports and the giant industrial processing complexes which dot the inland shores of those nations.

Here, too, the Coast Guards of two nations, the locks and channels of two nations, the pilots and seafaring men and the unions of two nations ply a common trade in virtually common waters. Giant corporations which own dozens of ore carriers larger than football fields, shipbuilding yards, a navigational system which is among the most sophisticated in the world — are among the bi-national threads out of which is woven the fascinating fabric of the merchant marine of North America's inland seas.

There are two types of maritime commerce in the lakes, really. One is inter-lake bulk commerce, and calls for the specialized vessel known as the *laker* or the *lake carrier*. The second is international trade, which travels to and from the remote ports of the world through the St. Lawrence Seaway, and to the deep-draft ports of both nations.[1]

The Great Lakes fleet today includes about 400 vessels with a total capacity of nearly 5,000,000 tons. About 57% is of U.S. registry, 43% Canadian. Ships are of various types and include bulk carriers of iron ore, grain, coal and stone, self unloaders, tankers, car carriers and cement carriers.

Two dominant organizations in the Great Lakes deal with the operational problems of most of the Great Lakes fleet. They are the U.S. Lake Carriers' Association and the Canadian Dominion Marine Association.

The Lake Carriers' Association was organized in 1892 as a successor organization to a Cleveland Owners Group, formed 12 years earlier. Throughout its existence, the Lake Carriers' Association has worked to reduce the hazards of lake navigation, to study environmental problems, to insure channel and harbor facilities for lake vessels, improve communication systems (including safety and distress signaling) and to promote the improvement of aids to navigation. The organization has been immensely strong in promoting winter navigation on the Great Lakes.

[1]This maritime activity is the subject of a companion book to *The Lake Carriers,* entitled *Seaway,* authored by Mr. LesStrang and published as a Salisbury Press book in 1976.

A Bateau (1755-1770), used for early transport in the region.

A Durham boat used in St. Lawrence River trade until about 1825. Most of the traffic along the St. Lawrence took place in this type of vessel.

Loading wheat at Chicago warehouses in 1839.

Vessel membership of some 159 ships includes bulk freighters, tankers and tugs, and barges documented under the laws of the United States. The vessels engage principally in the transportation of iron ore, coal, grain, petroleum products and cement.

Eighteen Canadian companies with a fleet of some 150 vessels including bulk carriers, self unloaders, package freighters and tankers comprise the Dominion Marine Association. The DMA fleet has a registered tonnage of 1.5 million and a carrying capacity of 2.5 million, representing an investment of more than $700,000,000. The fleet normally carries cargoes valued at $10,000,000,000 per year.

To help offset economic losses resulting from the winter season on the Great Lakes, many members of the DMA fleet are combined lakers/ocean vessels — ships designed to operate in salt water as well as fresh.

DMA was formed in 1903 when the shipping companies of Canada banded together for their interest represented by a single entity. Like the U.S. Lake Carriers' Association, Dominion Marine promotes navigational safety, high crew standards and operational practices and functions as a liaison with the Canadian government.

Also functioning in the Great Lakes maritime picture are some 50 companies which sail about 100 ships and which belong to neither the U.S. nor the Canadian marine associations.

If the development of Great Lakes shipping could arbitrarily be divided into two periods, the first would begin with the Indian canoe or the Bateau and the Mackinac Boat and run to the schooner and steamboat, ending with the early railroad competition in the 1850s. The second period would begin with the expanding rail competition and continue to today, with the advent of the land-locked, super-freighters.

As an early need for increased economy in operation was born in the Lakes, the maximum efficiency limits of the wooden ships were soon reached, and shipbuilders turned to iron for hull construction. While the wooden ships leveled out at about 350 ft., the iron vessels could be much bigger and, thereby, generated the revolution in shipbuilding which continues today.

The bulk cargo carriers of the Great Lakes — lake carriers — are unique in all the world. A highly specialized ship, the lake carrier was designed specifically to meet the conditions of the Great Lakes. Simply said, the flat sides of the vessel permit a tight fit into canal locks; long, unbroken hatch-covered decks permit on-shore loading and unloading equipment, or self-unloading equipment, built into the vessel, easy access to holds.

Typical lakers in service today vary in size and cargo capacity. Older vessels, built between 1910 and 1945, stretch about 600 ft. and carry around 14,000 tons of cargo. The more recently built lakers range from 670 to 730 ft. and carry about 25,000 tons. They make an 1800 mile round-trip from Lake Erie or Lake Michigan to the head-of-the-lakes and back in about five days. Ships up to 1,000 ft. long now are in use on the Lakes and have cargo capacities of more than 50,000 tons, and plans are underway for the construction of 1,100 vessels. (See Chapter VIII)

A typical laker carries between 28 and 40 men. The crew quarters define the configuration of the vessel. The wheelhouse is at the bow, the engine aft, with a long, flat deck designed for maximum efficiency in loading and unloading in between, and running the length of two or three — or more — football fields. Thus, the forward end of the vessel contains living quarters for the captain and the mates, wheelsmen and deck crew. The after end contains quarters for the chief engineer, his assistants and engine room personnel. The galley and dining rooms are also aft.

It was iron ore which built the Great Lakes fleet.

The waterborne movement of iron ore is the largest single commodity movement of all Great Lakes-St. Lawrence traffic. It accounts for over 45 per cent of all bulk traffic in the system. The ore movement alone from Lake Superior ports to lower lake ports, in fact, amounts to something like 80 million gross tons per year. The other three major commodities in Lakes bulk traffic are coal, grains and limestone, in that order.

Commerce through the St. Lawrence River section of the System is also dominated by bulk cargoes — ore and grains in particular — which represent about 70 per cent of total

The Hermaphrodite Brig, Ramsey Crooks *was built in Detroit in 1836 for service with the American Fur Company. The vessel was 100 feet long with a 28 foot beam and an 8 foot draft. The Hermaphrodite Brig carried the foremast of a brig and the main mast of a schooner. The main mast was made of two spars and carried no yards or square sails, with a square sail rig only on the foremast. This type of vessel required only a small crew.*

One of the first Great Lakes vessels to make a transoceanic voyage was owned by Canada Steamship Co. and traveled from Toronto to Liverpool and back in 1855. The drawing was made by the famous maritime artist, George A. Cuthbertson.

11

This romantic painting shows the Detroit River in
1872. A similar painting shows the Chicago River
during the same period, below.

The schooner Moonlight, *built at Milwaukee in 1874, is depicted in this romantic sketch.*

Seaway tonnage. Ore shipments through the international section of the Seaway originate in the Quebec-Labrador region and move up-bound to iron and steel producers through off-loading ports in Lakes Ontario, Erie and Michigan. The Welland Canal section of the St. Lawrence Seaway sees movements of ore in both directions.

From the standpoint of total tonnage, coal movement throughout the System is second in importance only to iron ore. The coal, used principally for power generation and in steelmaking, flows mostly from the U.S. ports of Lake Erie. The increased movement of low-sulphur coal from Duluth-Superior to the lower lakes and, in more recent export trade,

has added a new dimension to coal traffic in the System.

The movement of grain, wheat, corn, soy-beans, barley, oats and rye downbound through the St. Lawrence System accounts for the second major bulk commodity. Grain movements to domestic and export markets provide backhaul cargo for upbound ore vessels, which can return downbound fully laden either for off-loading at lower ports or for downriver St. Lawrence grain ports for the export market.

The movement of bulk cargo is undergoing rapid evolution in the Lakes. Many new self-unloaders, built with hopper holds and continuous belt conveyors, also carry rotatable

A fully-rigged Great Lakes vessel.

The last schooner to sail the Great Lakes was the Lucia A. Simpson, *built in 1875 and wrecked in 1929.*

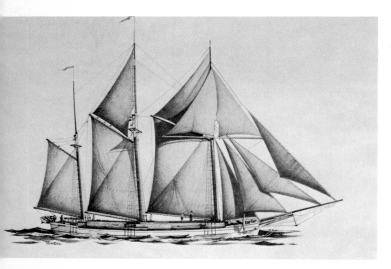

The J.V. Newland, *a swift Great Lakes schooner, carried 230,000 feet of lumber during the 1880s and '90s. The 120 foot vessel served from 1870 to 1937 and was one of over 3,000 similar sailing vessels to ply the Lakes during this era.*

above-deck structures which carry a conveyor and which, thereby, enable the continuous discharge of cargoes. (See Chapter VIII)

Many of these vessels were designed initially for the coal and limestone trades, but with the advent of taconite, self-unloading vessels have become immensely advantageous. All lake bulk vessels recently or currently under construction contain self-unloaders which, of course, allows for greater flexibility and speed in unloading and rapid turn around time.

At the same time, many older lake carriers are being refitted with unloading equipment and, at the same time, some are being "jumboized" — that is, cut in two and provided with a new mid-section to bring them up to a 730 ft. length.

Some vessels are being expanded at the expense of being able to operate east of Lake Erie — no longer able to transit the Welland.

Most bulk commodities handled within the Great Lakes trade are transferred at private terminals, so iron ore, coal, limestone, petroleum, cement and other bulk commodities are handled at terminals specifically designed for such cargoes. Logically enough, many bulk terminals are located near the industries that they serve and some, especially those dealing in coal and ore, are owned by the railroads that haul the commodities to the port hinterlands. Grain elevators are normally owned by cooperatives.

Andrew Carnegie once said that the northern portion of Ohio was the natural industrial center of the world for iron and steel. At no other point, he said, could iron ore and coal, both necessary for the manufacture of steel and iron, be assembled so economically as on the southern shore of Lake Erie.

Grain movement through the System is significant in that it is the one major volume commodity category which involves carriage by both the lake carriers and the ocean-going service. Grains move in both U.S. and Canadian domestic and international commerce.

Petroleum products moving through the System increase in importance each year, due to the energy shortages. Millions of tons of petroleum and related products now move through the St. Lawrence River section of the Seaway each year, with fuel oil as the pre-

The coal docks at Erie. Shown loading ore or already loaded and waiting to move out are the schooner John Schuette, *and* Queen of the West *with the schooner* Alice Norris *at her bow and the* Anna M. Peterson *with the* Camden *astern.*

dominant commodity. The major flow is from Canadian origins to the U.S. and Canadian destinations in the lower lakes.

Figures compiled on total bulk cargo movement on the Great Lakes during the thirties looked like this:

Year	Iron Ore	Coal	Grain	Stone	Total
1938	21,574,572	34,623,287	10,679,125	8,240,768	75,117,752
1937	70,110,696	44,318,765	5,829,399	14,429,379	134,688,239
1936	50,200,666	44,699,443	7,433,967	12,080,672	114,414,748
1935	31,765,852	35,289,135	6,750,261	9,082,155	82,887,403
1934	24,919,552	35,476,575	7,951,145	7,392,218	75,739,490
1933	24,218,766	31,776,654	8,713,127	6,664,629	71,373,176
1932	3,996,143	24,857,369	8,893,409	3,928,840	41,675,761
1929	73,029,152	39,254,578	10,021,099	16,269,612	138,574,441

Bulk tonnage, by 1975, had grown to these figures:

	Net Tons
Iron Ore	
From Lake Superior	74,592,958
	*(66,600,856)
From Lake Huron	1,296,816
	*(1,157,872)
From Lake Ontario	304,344
	*(271,736)
From Eastern Canada	13,248,631
	*(11,829,135)
	89,442,749
	*(79,859,599)
Bituminous Coal	
From Lake Erie	33,175,440
From Lake Michigan	3,943,165
From Lake Superior	2,061,426
	39,180,031
Anthracite Coal	
From Lake Erie	12,474
Grain	24,511,214
Limestone	35,876,608
	189,023,076

*denotes gross tons

Although experts seem to disagree, most tend to view two 922 ton vessels, the *Forest City* and the *R.J. Hackett,* each 213 ft. long and constructed of wood at Cleveland in 1869, as the prototype of the modern lake freighters — wheelhouse and engine fore and aft respectively, navigation quarters in the far forward foc'sl, and an uninterrupted cargo hold in between, on a flatsided hull. Still others point to the *Onoko,* launched in Cleveland 13 years later, as the first modern bulk carrier.

Whichever the case might be, the very first cargo vessels of any significant size to be built on the Great Lakes were constructed by the French between 1678 anbd 1759 and were the 10-ton *Frontenac,* the *Cataraqui* (20 tons) and *Le Generale* (10 tons), all built in 1678 at Fort Frontenac. The following year, the well-known 60-ton brigantine, the *Griffon* was built on Lake Erie.

It was the French explorer Rene Robert Cavalier, *Sieur de LaSalle* who cleared the site to lay the keel of the *Griffon* between Niagara Falls and Blackrock, New York. *Le Griffon* made her maiden voyage up the Niagara River toward Lake Erie with a party of 34 men, and in three days crossed all of Lake Erie, anchoring for provisions at the mouth of what is now the Detroit River. The tiny craft entered the waters of Lake Huron (where she was engulfed in a summer storm) then headed toward the Straits of Mackinac and into Lake Michigan, then called Lake Illinois by the Indians.

The trip ended at what is now known as Green Bay, where LaSalle loaded his ship with furs. He sent *Le Griffon* back home with cargo to satisfy his creditors. She was to return and pick up LaSalle and the remainder of his party, but another storm swept the lakes and *Le Griffon* was never seen again.

Well over a dozen other vessels — schooners, sloops and brigs — were built by the French at Fort Frontenac, Point au Baril and Fort Niagara during this period, while the British at Oswego, New York, between 1755 and 1756, constructed trading vessels which could carry between 60 and 172 tons and which were armed for service against the French.

What was known as the *Provincial Marine Fleet* operated in the Great Lakes until 1813. Under the control of the British Army Quartermaster General at New York and later in Canada, the fleet consisted of nearly fifty vessels: schooners, brigs, luggers, snows, sloops and one lateen.

Some were quite small, unnamed and built for specific service within a single lake. Others were staunch and proud, such as the 231-ton snow, *Ontario* (which was wrecked between Oswego and Niagara, New York with the loss of 120 members of the Kings Eighth Regiment aboard), or the *Haldimand* and the *Seneca,* 150 and 130-ton snows in Lake Ontario service.

The very first vessels to float on the waterways of the Great Lakes were the dugouts, canoes which the Indians called *Piroques.* Hollowed from logs, the huge canoes gave way in time to the *Birch bark canoe,* so well-known in the legends of the American Indian. These much lighter, more navigable canoes were used in commerce and ranged up to 35 ft. in length and five to six ft. in width. They were particularly suited to the north country and were used by earlier explorers who traveled the St. Lawrence and Ottawa Rivers to the upper lakes.

Probably the next boat in an informal chronology would be the *Bateau.* Made of flat pieces of wood sawed from red cedar logs and clipped or fastened together with iron bolts or wooden pegs, the flat bottom *Bateau* was reinforced with ribs and some *Bateaux* could carry nearly three tons of cargo. Three or four men were needed to propel the boat.

The *Mackinac Boat* came next and was the earliest of the barges used on the Lakes. It was constructed with a flat bottom of white oak boards and was well adapted to large cargoes. Because it was too unruly to paddle, the *Mackinac Boat* was towed or pulled.

In 1731, over 50 years after the *Griffon,* a Frenchman named LaRonde built the first of what was to become a new generation of sailing ships on the Great Lakes. It weighed nearly 40 tons and carried for the fur trade from LaPointe, the only port on the south shore of Lake Superior. In these early years of Lake navigation, only a few sailing vessels and smaller craft were owned by the French and English who controlled northwest trade. And it wasn't until 1789 that the first American vessels were built and rigged out for trade, these appearing first along the shores of Lake Ontario.

By the beginning of the second half of the 19th century, sailing vessels carried out a swift and profitable commerce on the Lakes. It often took only two shipping seasons for a ship to pay for itself with grain from Chicago and Milwaukee to Buffalo and Collinwood. And

Schooners (about 1880) discharge cargo.

the Lakes were busy. In a single day in 1873, for instance, over 130 schooners with cargoes of lumber were counted at Chicago.

The real growth of the Great Lakes fleet started about the time of the opening of the Erie Canal in 1825. Between the War of 1812 and the opening of the Canal, the Lakes fleet consisted primarily of sloops, brigs and schooners, with only slight displacement.

As both competition and technology developed, and as commerce called for larger and larger vessels, only the conditions of harbors and canals ultimately dictated maximum size for the vessels.

In 1860, steam appeared on the Great Lakes, and once less emphasis could be placed on vessel maneuverability in getting through rivers and into harbors, a drastic change appeared in the configuration of the Great Lakes fleet: vessels began to appear up to 200 ft. long, with a displacement of up to 800 tons.

A tabulation of the fleet in the upper lakes in 1870 listed 214 barques, 159 brigs and 1,737 schooners. These fleets served the fur trade as well as the forward movement of pioneers carrying all kinds of freight, including livestock, tools and household goods. In those days, grain moved west while down-bound cargoes, along with furs, included a variety of commodities.

The first vessels in Lake Ontario were trapped at either end — by rapids of the St. Lawrence River on the west and by the Niagara Falls at the eastern end. The Falls were bypassed with the first of the Canadian Welland Canals in 1829.

Although the schooners played the major role in Lake commerce until the early 1870s, the most accepted vessel, many marine historians claim, was the *barquentine*.

The barquentines were usually three masted, yet some were built with four or even five masts. This Great Lakes-designed vessel was easily managed in restricted waters and its popularity became so extensive that the configuration began to appear in the salt-water trades and were found as far away as India, Australia and South Africa.[2]

In building a ship for the Lakes, an owner had to first determine whether he wished to trade on the upper lakes or on all the Great Lakes and up the St. Lawrence River. If he wished to trade throughout the system, he was limited to the dimensions of the Welland

[2]There are only three conventional fully-rigged ships known to have been built for service on the Lakes — the *Superior*, the *Julia Palmer* and the *Milwaukee*.

Five lumber schooners are towed by a tug between Green Bay and Lake Michigan. They are the Charles E. Wyman, *the* Lyman M. Davis, *the* Iber Lawson, *the* Oscar Newhouse *and the scow,* Augustus. *The photo was taken in 1885.*

A traveling crane off-loads cargo from truck beds to the hold of a docked barge.

SPECIAL PHOTO SECTION I

The Imperial St. Clair, *a tanker in the Exxon service.*

The integrated tug-barge Presque Isle *(top). The self-unloading super-laker is constructed in two units with the power segment fitting into a notch to move the barge section of the combination. Together, they are one vessel.*

Off-loading a super-laker.

The U.S. Steel ore carrier Benjamin F. Fairless, *in fair weather and (below) in ice, getting an assist from the Coast Guard.*

Flying a flag to depict her test status, the Cleveland Cliffs' carrier Edward B. Greene *moves through the Great Lakes burning oil literally squeezed from shale rock.*

Canal, which restricted him to a vessel of 142 x 26 x 10 ft. These restrictions inadvertently developed a distinctive class of schooners, the early *Canalers*[3]: narrow ships with straight stems and flat transoms.

Lakers under sail during this period were easily distinguished from ocean-going sailing ships by their shoal-draft hulls, their square sterns, the straight-sided hull configuration, their short, broad mizzenmasts and, many, by their center-boards.

When the canal era began, the use of the center-board (invented by a Lieutenant Shank) was put into prominent use. The center-board was a thick oak plank weighted with lead or iron, running 10 to 15 ft. long and 6 to 10 ft. wide. It was housed in a water-tight box built from the keel onto the deck, with the keel and deck slotted to its width. A pivot at the forward end of the board allowed it to be hoisted or ducked at will. On leaving port, the center-board was lowered to provide vessel stability; upon entering the shallow canals, they were hoisted to allow passage.

Later on, a device called lightering was to be used to push cargo vessels through the Welland.

Even an increase of draft to 14 ft. through the Welland Canal severely restricted shipping into Lake Ontario and the St. Lawrence Valley. Harbors at both ends of the canal, however, did allow sufficient draft to accommodate large, fully loaded vessels.

To allow for cargo passage through the canal, the concept of lightering was introduced. The Grand Trunk Railroad constructed a line alongside the canal with elevators and switching tracks at each end of it. By transferring cargo to the railroads and transporting it overland, a vessel could be lightened sufficiently to meet the 14 ft. draft and pass through the Welland. At the other end, cargo was reloaded aboard and the vessel moved

[3]Another type of Canaler, much later, became a familiar sight in most of the ports of the Great Lakes, and along the Atlantic coast. These ships of shallow-draft with stubby stacks and low deck houses, built to navigate both in the Lakes and the oceans, were developed principally for cargo movement between the Eastern seaboard and Lake ports by way of the New York Barge Canal.

Our Son of Milwaukee – *built at Lorain in 1875 and sunk in Lake Michigan in 1930.*

Another view of Our Son. *This time the schooner is loaded.*

A lumber schooner pulls away from the docks at
Milwaukee around 1885.

upwards into the Lakes. This device was used until 1898 when inter-lake traffic went into a financial tailspin and transfer charges became unaffordable.

Much later, in 1907, only 93 vessels were lightered through the Welland Canal, of which 63 were Canadian steamers and tonnage totalled 1.6 million tons. In 1867, by contrast, 405 vessels passed through the Welland, carrying 933,263 tons.[4]

In 1841 the U.S. Congress set aside $100,000 to build armed vessels for the defense of the northwestern United States. The first iron vessel in the Great Lakes was put together at Erie and launched in December 1843.

The first merchant vessel to follow the new trend of iron construction was the Canadian *Richelieu*, a 167-ton, 130 ft. vessel put into service in 1845. The iron steamboat *Caspain* followed the next year, measuring 177 ft. and at 957 tons was followed in 1847 by the paddle steamer *Hamilton* and the steamer *Niagara*. The former was the same registry as the *Caspain* and the latter was 159 ft. and 369 tons.

By 1860 the Great Lakes fleet consisted of 138 steamboats, with a total tonnage of 69,150 tons, 197 propeller-driven craft with 67,550 tons, 122 sailing crafts of all classes with a carrying capacity of 252,152 tons.

The first iron merchant vessel under U.S. registry was propeller-driven and was put into service at 650 tons with 190 ft. length, 29 ft. beam and 14 ft. draft in 1861, at a cost of $60,000. In Canada, the *Quebec* was commissioned in 1865, and the following year, the *Canada*. The former iron vessel measured 282 ft. with a tonnage of 2,656. The latter was 248 ft. in length and registered at 1,768 tons. By 1871 the *Berthier* was added, and in 1871 the *Chambly* and *Terrebonne*, and the *Three Rivers* was added in 1847.

The Grand Trunk Railway constructed the iron paddle steamer, the *Huron* in 1875 to carry railroad cars across the Detroit and St. Clair Rivers, connecting their lines from the East via Canada. By 1880 about 20 American iron hulls were in service on the Great Lakes. The large iron steamers with submerged propellers were called "iron propellers". Four such early vessels of over 1,200 tons were the

Alaska, China, Japan and *India* and, beginning in 1871, carried cargoes between Chicago and Lake Erie ports.

Along with general cargo and grain, these vessels also carried passengers. The following year, the *Cuba* and the *Russia* were built and the steamer *Huron* was put into action in 1874. Five years later the side-wheeler *Adawild* and the propeller vessels *Leehigh* and *Boston* were added to the Great Lakes fleet. Although the trend was toward the iron hull ships, lower lake shipyards continued to turn out moderately-sized wooden vessels.

The sailing vessels on the Great Lakes reached their largest size in 1868 with a total of 1,859 registering 294,000 tons. The schooners, brigs, brigatines and sloops after this period began to decline, and by 1873, their number had dropped to 1,663.

During this period a unique, modified Great Lakes schooner appeared — a three masted vessel with a large square sail on the foremast in combination with a triangular *raffie*. This sail combination had never been seen before — or since.

The new era in the movement of heavy cargo actually occurred with the beginnings of the steamboat in the early 1860s. The first steam barges were built to fit the canals and were about 140 ft. in length, with a 26 ft. beam and 9 ft. draft. They registered about 250 tons net, and were largely used in commerce between the upper lakes ports, Ontario and the St. Lawrence River.

To compete with the steam barges, some schooners were connected to *tows*. The top masts and sails of these schooners were removed, their decks were cleared and several

---

[4]The Cleveland Steel Canal Boat Company in 1895, with a fleet of one steamer and five consorts (all steel canal boats), carrying 1,300 tons of steel, established a direct route from Cleveland to New York by way of the Erie Canal. The trip was made at such a low cost that others soon followed. The boats were 98 ft. long with an 18 ft. beam and up to 12 ft. draft. The steamer was built with 120 HP fore-and-aft compound engine and carried a 24" screw-type propeller. Well adapted and economical carriers on the canal, though they were, they could not withstand the open stretches of water between Cleveland and Buffalo (about 175 miles) and the experiment was soon abandoned.

A steam powered tug comes to the rescue of a trou-bled schooner.

ships were rigged together and towed by a tug. Acting essentially as barges, they could reasonably compete with the larger iron vessels.

A Captain James Norris of St. Catharines, Ontario was the first man to try this new technique. He hired a powerful American tug, the *Samson,* and tied up three of his schooners for a first tow to Chicago in 1869. Deck loads of cordwood on the schooners were used to fuel the tug and the caravan made a successful, fast round trip. Others soon followed his lead and more powerful tugs were put into service until it became commonplace to see schooners converted into tow barges.[5]

The big schooners, most of them, ended their days as tow barges behind tugs or steamers while the small schooner, which wrote the last chapter in the history of sail on the Great Lakes during the 1920s, lived on borrowed time in the coal and lumber trades.

By 1894 canal navigation had become considerably improved. One vessel emerged to shatter all previously known obstacles to Lake and ocean transportation. This was the barquentine *Eureka Cleveland* which left that port in the summer of 1849, heading for California. Operated by Mrs. W.A. Adair and Company, the *Eureka* sailed with 69 passengers up the St. Lawrence Canal to the Atlantic, where she rounded Cape Horn and entered the Pacific on her destination to San Francisco. The success of this voyage induced

[5]While passing into the Welland Canal, sailing ships had to wait for a tug to tow them to the lock, and as many as eight ships were bunched together to form a tow, with all sails tied.

others to follow, and in 1850 several other Great Lakes vessels headed out to sea.

A propeller-driven vessel, the 400-ton *Ontario,* was the first vessel to leave the Great Lakes for ocean navigation. The *Dean Richman* was the first to travel from Lake Michigan to Europe (1857), the same year the bark *C.J. Kerchaw* traveled from Detroit to Liverpool and the *Madiera Pet* also made the Detroit to Europe run. In 1858, 15 vessels traveled to Europe, and 16 did so the following year, sounding the beginning of foreign trade in the Great Lakes: in 1860, 39 vessels traveled down the St. Lawrence River to salt-water.

The steamer Onoko was christened in 1892 as the largest ship yet to sail the Great Lakes. Some 287 feet overall, she pioneered the use of iron hull construction in an era when other shipyards were still building wooden vessels. By her very design – the pilot house forward, the propulsion machinery aft and the long unobstructed cargo deck – the Onoko became the prototype of today's modern bulk carrier. In September 1915, the Onoko grounded while departing a Duluth grain elevator but freed herself and cleared the harbor; perhaps she sprung bottom plates, for suddenly water sprung through her engine room floor and when the vessel was off Knife River on Lake Superior, she settled stern first to the bottom, ending an historic career.

Types of Great Lakes Vessels

The bulk freighter first appeared in the 1880s, and within a decade evolved from wood to iron and steel construction. A major design in the transition to modern ore carrier came with the advent of the whaleback, a cigar-shaped ship 400 feet long, with a bow resembling a pigs snout. (The vessels, of course, were nicknamed Pig Boats.)

Typical lakers in service today vary both in size and in cargo capacities. Older steamers built between 1910 and 1945 are about 600 feet long—roughly the size of three football fields—and carry about 14,000 tons of cargo.

The more recently built lakers are between 670 and 730 feet long and carry up to 24,000 tons.

The super carriers, the 1,000 foot long vessels, now beginning to appear in numbers on the Lakes, have cargo capacities of around 50,000 tons. Most lakers have a long flat deck over holds with the wheelhouse, officers and deck crew cabins forward and the engine, galley, and engine room personnel quarters aft.

Ocean-going ships are cargo liners, tankers or bulk carriers. The cargo liner normally has cabins and engine rooms amidships, separated by cargo holds both forward and aft. Measuring up to 550 feet, the cargo liner normally carries general cargo—anything bagged, boxed, crated or bailed. Cargo capacity normally ranges up to 12,000 tons.

The ocean-going bulk carrier is often distinguished by having all machinery and cabins aft. This is a versatile ship of 500 to 700 feet which will handle grain and/or general cargo and which moves through the Great Lakes and into the Seaway system for its ultimate ocean voyage. Size, of course, is limited by the depth of channels and the dimensions of locks in the Seaway. Heaviest cargoes are in excess of 20,000 tons.

Early Great Lakes Chronology
(1500-1900)

1535   Jacques Cartier sails up the St. Lawrence River.

1615   Champlain discovers the Great Lakes.

1634   Jean Nicolet discovers Lake Michigan.

1668   Father Marquette founds a mission at the Soo.

1669   Lake Erie Discovered.

1670   The Hudson Bay Trading Company is founded.

1673   La Salle maps the Great Lakes.

1678   La Salle commences the first voyage on the Great Lakes.

1679   Sieur Du Lhut lands at Lake Superior site which is later named for him (Duluth).

        La Salle sets sail in the *Griffon*.

1701   Cadillac visits site of Detroit.

1790 Legislation approves creating the Revenue Marine—the present Coast Guard.

1798 Northwest Fur Co. builds first crude lock at the Soo.

1807 Robert Fulton sails on the Hudson River in first steamboat.

1813 Commodore Oliver Hazard Perry's victory in the War of 1812 at the Battle of Lake Erie gives U.S. rights to the lakes.

1815 Commercial activities begin on the Great Lakes.

1816 Work started on the Erie Canal; Steamer *Frontenac* launched in Lake Ontario.

1818 *Walk-in-the-Water,* launched at Black Rock, N.Y., is acclaimed as the first steamer on the Great Lakes.

First U.S. lighthouse on Lakes is built at Buffalo, N.Y.

1825 Work begins on the Welland Canal.

1829 Welland Canal opens for navigation.

1838 Ships screw propeller patented.

1845 First iron merchant vessel, the *Richelieu,* is built in Canada.

1847 St. Lawrence River canal system is completed, permitting ships to sail from lakes to the sea.

1850 Transportation boom started on the Great Lakes.

1855 First State Lock at the Soo completed.

1862 Steamer *Merchant,* pioneer iron freight ship, is begun.

1864 Era of sailing schooners on the Great Lakes.

1866 Michigan lumber shipping era begins.

1867 Big Sable Lighthouse is erected on Lake Michigan.

1868 Peak of sailing ship era on the Lakes.

1870 United States Weather Bureau is established.

1871 First coal cargo taken to Duluth.

1872 First ore development at Menominee Range.

1874 Little Sable Lighthouse on Lake Michigan is built.

1881 Weitzel Lock (No. 1) opens at the Soo.

1892 First Great Lakes car-ferry starts on Lake Michigan.

1893 Steamer *Christopher Columbus,* only whaleback passenger ship, is put in service.

1899 The Pittsburgh Steamship Company is forerunner of U.S. Steel Great Lakes Fleet.

The city ship canal at Buffalo Harbor, 1890.

Milwaukee shipyard, about 1880.

An interesting study of the after section of a lake carrier.

2

The Emergence of the Lake Steamer

The first 25 years of steam in the Great Lakes kept pace with the broad growth of the area, but as land speculation swept the Eastern states drawing people to the regions around the Lakes, the population explosion brought with it an expanding commerce, and the need for an expanding Great Lakes fleet of cargo and passenger vessels.

In 1836 there were 45 steamboats on the Great Lakes, weighing-in at 9,119 tons. There were 217 brigs and schooners with a combined weight of 16,645 tons. That year, the *United States* arrived at Detroit from Buffalo with 700 passengers. The following year, from Erie, came the *James Madison,* a steamer of 630 tons with the largest cargo capacity and accommodations for passengers of any ship on the Lakes.

The steamer *Nile* also entered the Great Lakes that year, as the Lakes fleet also saw the additions of the *New England,* the *Constellation, Bunker Hill, Buffalo, DeWitt, Clinton, Robert Fulton, General Wayne, Sandusky* and *Rochester.* The *Carolyn* and the *General Macey* came to the Lakes from the Hudson River (through the Erie Canal) to carry cargoes and help fulfill the needs of the growing population. In 1838, the *Illinois* was constructed at Detroit for the Chicago trade. She was over 250 ft. in length, with a 29 ft. beam and a 13 ft. draft.

By 1842 the Great Lakes fleet consisted of the following steamers: *Waterloo, Red Jacket, Chautauqua, Detroit, Swan, James Monroe, Baltic, Star, Lexington, Cincinnati, Arrow, Troy, Southerner, General Scott, Fairport, New Orleans, Ben Franklin, New York, Boston, Globe, Superior No. 2, Julius D. Morton, Champion, Sultana, Tecumseh, Little Erie,*

Constitution, Albany, Ohio, Vermilion, Baltimore, G.P. Griffith and *Saratoga.*

In 1846, on the Great Lakes there were 26 propeller driven vessels, 67 steamboats, 340 schooners, 64 brigs and three barques. The maximum vessel size was 350 ft. Cargoes consisted primarily of bulk commodities: stone, lumber, wood and coal. Tonnage for that year was approximately 107,000 of which over 60,000 tons was managed by steam and 46,000 on the sail Nearly 3.9 million tons of general cargo was transported, along with 250,000 passengers, involving some 7,000 sailors. Within a decade, the Great Lakes fleet had grown to 95 steamships, 45 propeller driven crafts, 93 brigs, 548 schooners, 128 sloops and skoals and five barques.

From Buffalo to Detroit the rate for cargo was 38¢ per hundred pounds for heavyweight and 50¢ for lightweight merchandise. The down-lake rates for flour from Detroit to Buffalo was 25¢, to which was added a charge of .05¢ a barrel for warehouse and elevator dues at these two terminals. Grain paid an .08¢ rate with an elevator rate of .02¢ a bushel. Meat and whiskey traveled at 10¢ per hundred pounds with an additional .03¢ charged at Buffalo.

Because westbound goods bound for ports on the upper lakes had to arrive before the close of the navigation season, they had to be ready to depart Buffalo by September 15.

By 1857 there were 107 sidewheel steamers, 135 propeller steamers and 1,006 sailing vessels of all classes on the Lakes. By 1868 the number of sailing vessels had grown to 1,875.

By 1880, the days of the sailing ship on the Great Lakes were waning, although there were still several thousand vessels engaged in

The American Eagle, *built in 1880 at Sandusky was 104 feet × 25 feet and for many years served as the "winter boat" for the Lake Erie Islands. Her white oak hull was known to have broken through 24 inches of solid ice. Converted to a tug in 1901, she burned several years later at Toledo. Her name lives on in Lake Erie in the American Eagle Shoal which her bottom accidently discovered in 1885.*

The steamer Sunbeam *was a wooden freight and passenger vessel built in 1861 for Capt. A.E. Goodrich of Chicago, the founder of Lake Michigan's Goodrich Steamship Lines, as an experimental ship. The vessel was originally called the* Victor *and equipped with a unique propulsion system that included two side mounted propellers. The machinery quickly proved a failure and the* Victor *was returned to the Bates Shipyard at Manitowoc, Wisc. where she was converted into a conventional sidewheeler and returned to service in 1862 bearing the name* Sunbeam. *She continued in service until 1863 when she was caught in a severe storm off the Keweenaw Peninsula on Lake Superior and floundered and sank.*

trade. The number reduced year by year and by 1900 only a few hundred were left. These were, as already noted, engaged principally in local runs.

A popular modified steam barge of the day was known as a *rabbit* — built with a high bow and a wheelhouse aft of the way station. Rabbits carried iron, stone, coal and often towed other vessels.

The *Railway Boat* was another type of late steamer to play an important part in the commerce of the Lakes. Owned by Eastern Railways and traveling the Chicago to Buffalo route, these vessels were distinguished by a huge truss which ran fore and aft on each side of the vessel, giving them the appearance of having been built around a section of railroad bridge.

The *Lumber Hooker* was another unique Great Lakes vessel. Normally under 200 ft. and made of wood, the hooker was used to bring lumber from the northern lakes to Cleveland and other lower lake ports. When the lumber trade was slack, hookers carried pulp wood, paper and sometimes coal. Popular in the '90s, they disappeared with the northern forests.

To any list of early lake carriers, of course, must be added the railroad transports — vessels in competition with other types of water transport, linking rails between opposite banks of the Lakes. The main deck of a rail transport was usually for box car space, with, normally, four tracks running lengthwise and the loading and unloading end of the vessel at the stern instead of the bow, as is the case with other ferries. The hull, 17 ft. above this deck, extended to the end of the bow. An upper deck was filled with state rooms, dining salons and conveniences for passenger traffic. Above the upper deck were officer's cabins, pilot house, life boats and other facilities.

Most rail-link traffic flowed from Michigan to Manitowoc and Milwaukee and Kewaunee. Another route operated between Muskegon and Milwaukee.

The largest of the railroad fleets was the *Pere Marquette,* which kept six transports in action, along with four large freight and passenger steamers. On Lake Michigan, in addition to the *Pere Marquette,* car ferries were run by the Ann Arbor Railroad, the Lake Michigan Car Ferry Transit Company, Grand Rapids and Indiana Railroad, Grand Trunk and the Mackinac Transportation Company.

On Lake Erie, the Marquette-Bessemer Dock and Navigation Company operated four vessels; the Ann Arbor operated four; the Lake Michigan Car Ferry operated two; Grand Rapids and Indiana operated three; the Grand Trunk operated one; and the Mackinac Transportation Company operated two. Another important car ferry route was established in 1907 between Ashtabula and Port Barwell, Canada.

The Anchor Line was well-known throughout the Lakes as the water operating arm of the Erie and Western Transportation Company—which was later to be known as the Pennsylvania Railroad. Anchor controlled 15 steamers, with over 60,000 tons of cargo capacity. The Western Transit Line operated a fleet of 16 package freighters between Buffalo and Chicago and Duluth, carrying a total of 65,000 tons on a single trip.

The Mutual Transport Company, controlling the Union Steamship Line, was the

The Wolverine, *an early sidewheeler.*

operating arm of the fleets of the Great Northern and Northern Pacific Railroad. It consisted of 15 vessels in the upper lakes trade, with a cargo capacity of close to 70,000 tons.

The Lehigh Valley Transit Company was another major railroad-controlled shipping line which owned six large steel freighters that worked the Duluth, Chicago, Buffalo route in connection with the Lehigh Railroad Company, by which they were owned.

The first sidewheelers appeared early in the 19th century. Two sidewheelers, the *Dalhousie* and the *Accommodation,* operated on the St. Lawrence River in 1809 and a steamboat built at Black Rock called *Walk In the Water,* a passenger and freight carrier, was launched in 1818. The latter vessel was a cross between a steamer and a sailing craft, carrying two high masts and fitted with a square rigged foresail. The smoke stacks stood between the masts. Two paddle boxes which housed their paddlewheels were placed exactly midships. She was about 150 ft. in length with 30 ft. beam and eight ft. draft with a gross tonnage of 338 tons. Her bow carried a figurehead of Commodore Oliver Perry.

The steamboats received their impulses from an open, double-spoked rimless perpendicular wheel at each side of the vessel. To the end of each double spoke was fixed a square board which enters the water, and by a rotary motion of the wheel, acted like a paddle. The wheels were operated by steam from within the vessel.

Sail and steam powered the Wolverine.

APRIL 9-1865

Fleet of over a hundred canal barges at Chicago waiting for the opening of navigation in April, 1865.

The Montauk *came to the Lakes in 1902 as an excursion vessel and served until 1939. The big iron sidewheel steamer later was converted into a barge and remained in the Lakes until she was abandoned at Bay City, Michigan around 1970.*

The first ore boat to enter the Port of Conneaut arrived November 18, 1892. She was the Charles A. Kershaw. *She carried 130 tons and was unloaded in a record 72 hours.*

A mast was often fitted to the steamboat for the use of sail when the wind was favorable.

In the nine years following the construction of the *Dalhousie* and the *Accommodation,* several riverboats were built, including the *Swift Sure, Car of Commerce, Caldonia, New Swift Sure, Malsham, Lady Sherbrooke, Telegraph* and *Quebec the First.*

The advent of the screw-type propeller on the Lakes occurred in 1841 on Lake Ontario. The vessel *Vandalia,* 138 tons, was the first vessel on the Lakes to use the propeller. The compactness of the mechanism to drive the propeller diminished the need for fuel, creating additional area for cargo.

The second prop-type vessel, the *Oswego,* was built in 1842 for service on Lake Ontario. Another propeller-driven vessel in the era was the *Hercules,* a 273-ton vessel equipped with twin screws. Through 1843 the *Chicago, New York* and *Racine* were constructed at Oswego and supplied with screws and engines the same type as the *Hercules. The Independence, Samson, Immigrant* and vessels with larger propellers soon followed, such as the *Syracuse* and *Phoenix,* all 350 tons.

By mid-century, 50 propeller-type vessels, totalling nearly 6,500 tons began replacing the sidewheelers. At this time the *California, Goliath, Manhatten* and *Globe* joined the fleet.

General Charles M. Reed of Erie, Pennsylvania brought together in the 1840-50 era one of the first fleets of the Great Lakes. More than

25 vessels, mostly sidewheelers, were owned, operated or chartered by Reed, including some of the better-known vessels of the time. The Marine Historical Society of Detroit has placed over 20 of these steam-driven vessels. The list includes the following:

Albany, wooden sidewheeler, built in 1866 at Detroit, 669 tons.

Baltic, 1847 Buffalo, wooden sidewheeler, 225 × 30 × 12.5, 825 tons.

Buffalo, 1838 Buffalo by J. Carrick. Launched as *Manhattan,* but registered as *Buffalo.* 189 × 28 × 12, 613 tons.

Chesapeake, 1828 Maumee City, Ohio. Wooden sidewheeler, 172 × 25 × 10, 412 tons.

Empire, 1844 Cleveland. Sidewheeler, 255 × 33 × 14, 1136 tons.

Empire State, 1848 St. Clair, Mich. Originally 298 × 37 × 14, 1553 tons. Lengthened to 314 ft. in 1851, 1691 tons.

Erie, 1837 Erie, Pa. by Creamer. 176 × 26 × 10.

Globe, 1848 Trenton, Mich. by J. Robinson. 251 × 34 × 15. Sidewheeler but soon converted to a propeller.

Hendrik Hudson, 1846 Cleveland by G. W. Jones. Sidewheeler, 202 × 32 × 12, 750 tons.

Thomas Jefferson, 1834 Erie by S. Jenkins. 174 × 27 × 10, 428 tons.

Keystone State, 1849 Buffalo. 279 × 35 × 14, 1354 tons.

Louisiana, 1846 Buffalo. Sidewheeler with engines from the *Thomas Jefferson.* 224 × 29 × 12, 777 tons.

James Madison, 1837 Presque Isle (Erie), Pa. Sidewheeler with high pressure engine. 178 × 31 × 13.

Michigan, 1847 Detroit. 190 × 28 × 11, 647 tons.

Missouri, 1840. Conflicting data shows both Erie, Pa. and Vermilion, O. as place of build. Sidewheeler, 612 tons, later changed to propeller.

Ohio, 1847 Ohio City, O. by L. Moses. Sidewheeler, 583 tons.

A.D. Patchin, 1846 Truago, Mich. Sidewheeler with side lever engines from *Missouri.*

Queen City, 1848, Buffalo. Sidewheeler, 242 × 35 × 13, 906 tons.

Rochester, 1838 Richmond City, Ohio (near present Fairport). Sidewheeler with high pressure engine, 472 tons.

St. Louis, 1844, Perrysburg, Ohio. Wooden sidewheeler, 190 × 27 × 12, 618 tons.

Sultana, 1846 Angonac, Mich. wooden sidewheeler, 217 × 30 × 12, 806 tons.

In this hey-day of the Great Lakes—the mid-80s—the largest class of lake passenger steamers—day or excursion types—operated from 10 to 15 weeks in the summer, and during that time, they were usually crowded to full capacity. The passenger ship was, indeed, the queen of the Lakes, beautifully fitted with elegant and ornate cabins, fine food, orchestras and tranquil passages.

Five propeller vessels served Buffalo and Detroit runs with three steamers between Detroit and Dunkirk, the terminal of the Erie railroad to New York; three between Detroit and Cleveland; one between Detroit and Sandusky; two between Detroit and Toledo and one between Detroit and Chatham, Ontario. There were also many scheduled passenger runs between major Great Lakes ports.

Passenger rates for cabin passage from Buffalo to Detroit were $8.00; Buffalo to Cleveland $6.00, and to Chicago, Green Bay or St. Joseph $20.00. In 1879 a run between Buffalo and Chicago was a 16-day turn around.

The passenger service sharply stimulated the shipment of merchandise, resulting in somewhat of a revolution in the construction of ships—with the *Great Western* as the prototype.

This vessel put passengers on an upper cabin deck, allowing lower or main deck to be used for additional freight. When it became apparent that the *Great Western* performed well with its upper deck concept, the owners of other steamships reconstructed their vessels, adding opulent upper passenger decks. The *Niagara, Louisiana, Indiana, Empire State, City of Buffalo, St. Louis, Wisconsin, Missouri, Columbus* and *Angelo Harrison* were all fitted out in this manner. In 1841, six of the largest combination vessels earned over $300,000.

The passing of the years saw the sidewheelers in the Great Lakes shoved aside by the expanded cargo capacity and lower operating costs of more sophisticated power driven vessels. The whaleback introduced a unique era of steam to the Great Lakes in the 1890s, simultaneously creating one of the most vividly colorful eras in Great Lakes shipping.

A Captain Alexander McDougall invented and built his whalebacks, for the most part, at the American Steel Barge Company's shipyard in West Superior, Wisc. In his autobiography, McDougall tells of the events leading up to the whaleback:

"While Captain of the Hiawatha, towing the Minnie Ha Ha and Goshwak through the difficult and dangerous channels of our rivers, I thought out a plan to build an iron boat cheaper than wooden vessels. I first made plans and models for a boat with a flat bottom designed to carry cargo into these waters with a rounded top so that water could not stay on board, with bow shaped to best hold the line of strain with the least use of the rudder and with turrets on deck for passage into the interior of the hull."

The first model, *No. 101,* a barge, he made on his own land at Duluth, with stevedore labor. He loaded it with ore at Two Harbors for a tow to Cleveland.

In 1889, came *No. 102.* McDougall arranged for financial backing with John D. Rockefeller interests. A company was subsequently formed, named the American Steel Barge Company, which made *No. 103.* The steamer, *Colgate Hoit* was next, named for McDougall's

SPECIAL PHOTO SECTION II

The Upper Lakes Shipping, Ltd. vessel, Canada Century *and below, the* McKee Sons, *two splendid examples of Great Lakes self-unloaders.*

These four photographs show industrial loading by Hulett. Upper right, the U.S. Steel vessel *Eugene W. Pargny, a taconite carrier, is seen at the loading* docks. A closer view (below) shows the gaping jaws of a Hulett unloader approaching the open hold of the vessel.

The photo on top shows the Hulett above the hold, actually driven by the operator who can be seen through the window in the Hulett's shaft. The photo below shows the Hulett in the hold, scooping up taconite for off-loading.

The Incan Superior *(above) transports freight cars. Below the* St. Clair, *of the Canadian National Service, does the same thing.*

Whalebacks, also known as pig boats because of their protruding snouts, in 1893.

Rockefeller associate and financial backer. In 1890 McDougall was employing 1,000 men.

The keel and bottom of the whalebacks were carried port to a point 100 ft. forward on a curve and terminating in the "snoot" high above the waterline. Thirty feet beyond this point was a low lookout turret, and within the turret was located the gear necessary at the bow.

The deck was clear and held many hatches to expedite cargo handling. Engines and boilers, coal bunkers or steam steeling gear were located in the far stern, behind a watertight bulkhead. Above the main deck, supported by another turret was the wheelhouse and chart room. A small tunnel passed through the turret behind which was located crew quarters and galley.

The Clermont, *outfitted with sail and steam.*

Fully loaded whalebacks.

"In 1893 we built 10 steel ships at once . . ." McDougall wrote. *"That year we launched a ship every Saturday for eight Saturdays and on the next Saturday launched two ships and a tug. We also built the World's Fair steamer, the Christopher Columbus (a whaleback passenger ship), probably the most wonderful ship contracted for and constructed up to this time."*

In the ten years between 1888 and 1898 McDougall built 46 whalebacks.

Ore, compactly stored in the unique holds, actually helped the vessels in bad wheather. When the Mesabi range opened in Minnesota, a long-term contract tied the whaleback fleet into ore carrying to Lake Erie ports. At this point, however, oblique legal problems caught the whaleback fleet in the middle of court battles and the vast ore carrying potential of the boats were never really fulfilled.[6]

An interesting sidelight in U.S.-Canadian relations — normally peaceful and cooperative — occurred in the 1880s when Canada attempted to compel United States grain exporters using the Welland Canal to ship their cargoes overseas through Montreal. They did this by imposing a toll of 20¢ a ton on all U.S. cargoes transiting the Welland, with cargoes that were subsequently exported through Montreal receiving a rebate of 18¢ a ton. Understandably, United States shipping interests resented this maneuver, and Congress passed a law that provided, *"all freight passing through the United States' Soo locks in transit to any port in Canada"* should pay retaliatory tolls in certain circumstances, and a total of 20¢ a ton on Canadian cargoes was imposed.

Naturally, Canada protested the tolls, claiming they were contrary to the spirit of an earlier treaty signed in 1871. The United States refused to abolish the toll, however, until Canada agreed to abolish their tolls on the Welland in 1901. Thereafter, all of the inland waterways of North America were toll free until the opening of the Seaway in 1959.

The "St. Marys Falls Canal Statute" is still on the books, and still stands as a device which the United States could, if it wanted, use in a toll battle with Canada.

During this same period of time, the era of steel ship construction began in the Great

[6]The legal battles existed between the interests of John D. Rockefeller and Andrew Carnegie. They were solved by the creation of the U.S. Steel Corporation, combining the interests of both parties.

Lakes. The Pittsburgh fleet[7] included a 290 ft. vessel, the *Cambria,* and the following year, the *Coronna* and *Corsica,* 312 ft., were added. In 1891, the *Briton, German, Rowen* and *Saxon,* of the same dimensions, were built. Six vessels of the 400 ft. class were built in 1898 with 1,225 and 1,450 ft. vessels — steamers and barges built up to 1898.

In 1871 the U.S. Supreme Court declared that all upper lakes, including Lake Erie, were seas—commercially and legally. Congress, as a result of this decision, was empowered to improve the harbors of the lakes and channels, just as it did at tidewater ports. Ever since, the Corps of Engineers has dredged channels to keep the shipping lanes open in the Great Lakes.

Early marine construction by the Corps included a crossing through the western delta of the Detroit River, the expanded canal locks at the Soo and improvements to harbors and rivers from Superior to Erie and including the dredging of ports on Lake Michigan.

In keeping with the legislation, light ships and lighthouses were also installed in the Lakes to mark shoals, dangerous coasts and reefs. Buoys, bells and beacons were dropped in river and harbor channels. Lifesaving stations were installed and weather reporting installations.

The installation and maintenance of lighthouses in the Great Lakes at that time was under the direction of a Lighthouse Board, composed of the Secretaries of the Treasury, Army and Navy. Lighthouses, until then, had been under the control of the Fifth Auditor of the Treasury Department. The Lighthouse Board maintained nearly 2,000 aids to navigation, both fixed and floating. In addition, the Board controlled over 100 bell or whistling fog signals and large numbers of buoys.

The great lighthouses, such as Spectacle Reef, were astonishing engineering feats. This particular rock lies in the northern part of Lake Huron, near the entrance to Mackinac, 10 miles away from land. It is directly on a route for vessels heading through the Straits, near the course of the St. Marys River and Lake Superior.

[7]Later to be known as the U.S. Steel Great Lakes Fleet, largest of the lake carriers.

The ferry Miss Vandenburg *leaving her berth at Prescott, Ontario. Built in 1909 for the Ogdensburg-Prescott Ferry Company, the vessel is believed to be among the first motorships to be constructed. Because of the type of fuel she burned the vessel was nicknamed "Kerosene Annie."*

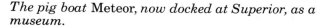

The pig boat Meteor, *now docked at Superior, as a museum.*

The structure was completed in 1873, built by the Corps under General Orlando M. Poe, Chief Engineer of the Corps and designed by General William T. Sherman of Civil War fame, whose many efforts throughout the Great Lakes bear vivid witness to his abilities.

On the other side of the border, the first lighthouse was established at Chipwater Point, Lake Ontario, in 1798. This mighty rectangular shaped tower was 80 ft. from ground to lantern gallery.

In order to pay for the construction and maintenance of lighthouses, an act was passed by the Legislature of Upper Canada in 1803 taxing all vessels of 10 tons or more 3¢ per ton per voyage.

Also in 1803, the Mississauga Point Light, at the entrance to the Niagara River, was begun. This was a six sided masonry tower 60 ft. from the ground to lantern gallery. After the U.S. Congress OK'd the use of federal funds for the erection of lighthouses on the Great Lakes, two were begun on Lake Erie; the Buffalo Harbor Light at Buffalo and the Erie Harbor Light at Erie, Pa. These were the first two lights to go into operation on the U.S. side of the Lakes.

In 1820 the Galleau Island Light was constructed at the eastern end of Lake Ontario

Whaleback ore vessels provide sharp contrast to more conventional ore boats at right, Circa 1895.

The first Welland Canal, showing a remnant of the old wooden lock wall.

and, in 1823, the Port Niagara Light was installed at the eastern bank of Lake Ontario. The Gratiot Light was established on Lake Huron at the entrance to the St. Clair River in 1825 and in 1832, the Chicago Light.

In 1837 on the Detroit River, the Windmill Point Light was constructed and the first U.S. floating light ship on the Lakes was put into service at the Straits of Mackinac between Lakes Michigan and Huron.

The Canadians, up to this point in time, had also established a number of lights, beacons, buoys and other markings on Lake Ontario, Erie, Huron and on the St. Lawrence River. In 1847 the Whitefish Point Light was established as the first light on Lake Superior and by 1848 the Copper Harbour Light, and by 1850, the Eagle Harbour Light were estab-

lished in Lake Superior. The Ontonagon Light, also on Lake Superior, was constructed in 1852. In 1853 the Marquette Harbor Light was put up in Lake Superior.

Control of all Canadian lights and buoys were taken over by the government at Ottawa in 1868, and in 1903 the U.S. Lighthouse Board was transferred to the U.S. Dept. of Commerce.

The Great Lakes Canals — An Early Chronology

No work on the Great Lakes fleet would be complete without at least a brief look at the early history of the major canals of the system. A chronology of events and improvements involving the four most significant ones—St.

47

The size of the whaleback was often deceiving, and not until people put it into scale was the dimension of these giants really appreciated.

Welland Ship Canal, Lock No. 1 in 1951. Note gate lifter.

Lawrence, St. Marys (Sault Ste. Marie), Welland and the Erie would include the following:

St. Lawrence Canals (Canadian)

1698   Proposal to build bateau canal between Montreal and Lachine proposed by Dolier du Casson.

1770   The Royal Engineers began work on four canals: Coteau du Lac, Cedars, Cascades Point and Split Rock Channel. The locks were 40 × 6 with a depth of 30″ over the sills.

1783   The four canals opened for navigation.

1800   Enlargement and merging of Coteau du Lac and Cascades Point Canals begun by the Royal Engineers at the request of the Lower Canada Legislature. Locks increased from six to 10 ft. wide with 3½ ft. depth over the sills and four ft. in the channel.

1806   Completion of clearances at Lachine Rapids.

1825   Lachine Canal opened for navigation. The canal consisted of a main channel and 12 locks, built of stone, 100 ft. long, 25 ft. wide and five ft. depth over the sills, with a channel depth of five feet.

1843   Completion of the Cornwall Canal: 1½ miles long, with a channel 100 ft. wide and a nine foot depth. Seven 100 ft. locks with widths of 25 ft. and depth over the sill of nine feet.

1847   Work on canals at Farran's Point, Beauharnois, Galops and Point Iroquois was completed. All were nine feet at lock sills, 100 ft. locks and a channel width of 90 ft.

1868   All Canadian canals taken over by federal government.

1871   Improvement began to provide a uniform draft of 12 ft. (later changed to 14) at Welland and St. Lawrence Canals. Locks were to be 207 ft. long (changed to 270 ft.) and a width of 45 ft. Channels and approaches were also to be enlarged.

1901   Completion of navigation program begun in 1871.

The Welland Canal (Canadian)

1821   Preliminary surveys for a canal route made by William Merritt and Captain de Cou.

1824   Welland Canal Company formed.

1825   Work began on the canal, from Twelve Mile Creek on Lake Ontario (Port Dalhousie) to its source on the Niagara Escarpment, where a connecting channel was to be made to the Chippewa River. Lock dimensions were 100 ft. (later changed to 110 ft.), width 22 ft. and depth over the sills of eight ft.

1829   Canal opened for navigation.

1833   Canal extended from Port Robinson on the Chippewa, to Port Colbourne on Lake Erie.

1841   Canal Company purchased by the Upper Canadian Legislature. Work started to enlarge the canal and rebuild the locks.

1868   All Canadian canals taken over by the government.

The second Welland Canal, St. Catharines, Ont.

1871 Improvement program begun to provide uniform navigation on Welland and St. Lawrence Canals.
1887 Completion of 1871 lock and channel improvements. Fourteen foot navigation.
1927 The peak year for traffic through the Canal during the early decades—7.2 million tons. (In 1901, when the St. Lawrence Canals were first opened to 14 ft. vessels, traffic was 620,000 tons.)
1929 Work underway on 27.7 mile ship canal, 27.7 miles long, with a lift of over 320 ft. between Lake Ontario and Lake Erie, locks 820 ft. long, width 80 ft. and depth over the sills of 30 ft.

Sault Ste. Marie Canals (U.S.)

1798 Canal for boats and canoes completed by the Northwest Company on Canadian side of the St. Marys River. This ditch terminated in a lock 38 ft. long, 8¾ ft. wide with a depth over the sills of 30 inches and a lift of 9 ft.
1814 Lock and canal destroyed by U.S. troops.
1816 Lock and canal rebuilt.
1823 Tramroad built on the U.S. side of the river by the American Fur Company.
1837 Act passed by the Michigan Legislature to build a ship canal with three locks to overcome the 18 ft. lift. The locks were to be 100 ft. long, two ft. wide and 10 ft. deep over the sills with a channel 75 ft. wide and 10 ft. deep. Total estimated cost was to be $112,000.
1852 Captain Canfield of the U.S. Army Corps of Engineers appointed as Chief Engineer for Canal works. Canal was to have two locks, each with a nine ft. lift, 350 ft. long, 70 ft. wide and with a depth over the sills of nine ft. A channel 5,400 ft. long and 100 ft. wide was to be built from the upper river to lead into the locks.
1855 Canal completed and opened on June 18 when S.S. Illinois passed up into Lake Superior. In the same year, the brigantine Columbia passed down with the first iron ore cargo. The Canal cost the State of Michigan $100,000.

1870 Canal enlargements approved by the State for an additional single lift lock 515 ft long, 80 ft. wide and having 16 ft. depth over the sills.
1881 Weitzel Lock completed at a cost of $2,200,000. A third lock projected; Canal taken over by the U.S. Government.
1887 Work begun on the third lock, known as the Poe Lock: 800 ft. long, 100 ft. wide and 18 ft. deep over the sills.
1890 Canadian government began construction of a lock on the north side of the river.
1895 Canadian and Poe locks opened for traffic. The Canadian lock is 900 ft. long, 60 ft. wide and has a depth over the sills of 18 ft. 2 in.
1907 Second canal started on the Michigan side with two locks, Sabin and Davis: each are 1350 ft. long, 80 ft. wide and have a depth over the sills of 24½ ft.
1914 Davis Lock opened.
1919 Sabin Lock opened.

The Erie Canal (U.S.)

The Erie was not nearly as important to the Great Lakes as it was to New York State. At one time considered an alternate or additional route to the St. Lawrence River, the Erie once again is under study by the Corps of Engineers as an additional access from the Lakes to the sea.

1817 Canal construction started at Hudson River.
1825 Canal opened for navigation between Lake Erie and the Hudson. The waterway was 363 miles long and overcame a difference in level between Lake Erie and the Hudson of 568 ft. by means of 83 locks and 18 aqueducts.
1826 Schooner St. Clair first Great Lakes canal sailing vessel to navigate to the sea via the Erie Canal.
1899 Enlargement proposed for Erie Canal.
1916 New Canal fully completed. As rebuilt, the canal had a length of 339 miles (Waterford on the Hudson to Tonawanda on the Niagara, at Lake Erie). A branch was constructed to

The third Welland Canal looking southwest from Lock 17, July 1925.

Oswego on Lake Ontario 24 miles long. Thirty-six locks in the main canal, eight in the Oswego branch, all uniformly 328 ft. long, 45 ft. wide, with 12 ft. over the sills. The channel width averaged 123 ft. and had a depth of 12 ft.

Characteristics of Major Great Lakes Vessel Types

Vessel Types	Length (ft.)	Beam (ft.)	Draft (ft.)*	Cargo Tonnage	Employment
Pre-Seaway "Canaller" (Lake service)	258	43.5	14.00	3,000	Great Lakes-St. Lawrence[1] Pre-Seaway Canal System
Pre-Seaway "Canaller" (Lake-Overseas Service)	258	43.5	14.00	1,600[2]	Great Lakes-Overseas Direct via Pre-Seaway Canal System
Cuyahoga River Laker	630	68.0	25.75	18,000	Great Lakes, St. Lawrence[3]
"Maximum Laker" (pre-1970; post-1959)	730	75.0	25.75	28,000	Great Lakes, St. Lawrence west of Sept. Isles, Quebec
"Maximum Laker" (post-1970)	1,000	105.0	25.75	57,500	Great Lakes, west of Welland Ship Canal
Typical Great Lakes-Overseas General Cargo Liner	500	75.0	24.00	9,000	Great Lakes-Overseas Direct
Typical Lake-Ocean Bulk Carrier	600	75.0	25.75	25,000	Irregular Great Lakes-Ocean Service

NOTE: *Maximum draft normally allowed for transit of lock system.

[1]Obsolete since opening of enlarged Seaway System in 1959.
[2]On Seaway draft; additional 1,000 tons on 18 foot draft east of Montreal.
[3]Dimensions limited by Cuyahoga River at Cleveland, Ohio.

**Source: Great Lakes Transportation System: Schenker, Mayer and Brocko, University of Wisconsin, College Program, 1975.

51

The ore docks at Superior, Wisconsin, with five vessels being loaded with coal. In the foreground is the J. Emory Owen; *at right is the* Polynesia *and directly behind her, the* Wolverine.

3

The Early Giants

In 1898 a 475 ft. vessel was built at the shipyards at Bay City and nine others of this class soon followed. By the close of the century, the 500 ft.-class steamer came into being with a 10,000 ton cargo capacity. In 1905 four 569 ft. vessels were built and in 1906 the 600 ft. giant lake carrier came into her own: the new monolith of the Lakes.

While the Pittsburgh fleet was dominant during that period, the Gilcrest fleet was also importantly engaged in general trade. This fleet consisted of 34 steel vessels and 35 wooden ones, all steamers except five, which were barges. The Pittsburgh Steamship Company carried a roster of 105 vessels, of which 78 were steamers, 27 were barges and schooners. The total registered tonnage of this fleet was 200,000 and the cargo carrying capacity more than 1/3 million tons on a single trip.

Also on the U.S. side, 19 steamers, 16 of which were steel, were operated by Mitchell and Company and the U.S. Transit Company operated 12 steel freighters, registering 51,500 tons. The Mitchell fleet registered 80,000 tons. Twelve vessels were owned by the Cleveland-Cliffs Company, registering 37,000 tons.

The Hawgood fleet consisted of 11 steamers, (none of which were steel) with a registry of 48,700 tons. Seven Hutchinson freighters registered 30,000 tons and the Wilson Transit Company operated seven steamers of steel with 28,000 tons total. Pickands Mather and Co. had 11 vessels and the fleet of James Corrigan had 11 vessels of various sizes, registering 23,000 tons. The Provident Steamship Company operated three large freighters at 15,000 tons and other lines owning ore carriers included Jones and Laughlin, two; the L.C. Smith, one; and the Cambria Steel Company, two. Several other large vessels were built under a bonding plan and were operated independently.

During the first decade of the 20th century, more than one third of all American tonnage was represented by Great Lakes shipping. In that period, there were some 75 vessels with a total of 300,000 tons capacity, including fourteen 600 ft. ore carriers with 20,000 tons capacity and a 24 ft. draft.

During this time, the draft along the Detroit River, the St. Clair channels and in the St. Marys River was only about 20 ft. and so the carrying capacity of these carriers was reduced to something like 14,000 tons of ore or 400,000 bushels of grain.

When one of the early 600 ft. vessels was launched—the *J. Pierpont Morgan*—its Captain noted that in order to carry as much ore from Duluth to Cleveland as he would carry on his first trip, it would take two and a half years on the first steamer he had commanded two decades earlier.

The new 600 ft. ore carriers were more correctly suited to requirements for Lake service than any other type of vessel. With an ore chute at each of her hatches, the largest carrier could load in two hours and no more than 10 hours were required with unloaders to clear the hold. In Superior, a freighter could take 5,250 gross tons of cargo in 30 minutes—at a rate of 10,000 tons an hour. And even these records were quickly broken as new equipment was designed and constructed to serve the long boats.[8]

[8]A tongue-in-cheek rule for defining vessel size has always been that a boat is something you take to get a ship. But in the Great Lakes, the giant lake carriers are more often than not called "boats," just as speeds, rather than being measured in knots, are calculated in shore miles-per-hour.

The steamship J.H. Macoubrey *coming down through the lower Detroit River.*

The Interlake Steamship Company's Augustus Wolvin *in Lake Michigan.*

The carrier Harvard.

The tug W.A. Roote *of Port Colborne and other vessels assist the sunken* Douglas Houghton, *a sunken carrier.*

The David Z. Norton – *an early carrier.*

Fleet of barges at Lock 11, Tribe Hill, New York.

Lake Storms, especially in Lake Superior, are often very violent before the close of the season and lake ships must be able to head into a storm and fight it out, rather than run from it. This means that a freighter lying deep in the water will be awash amidships with the bow often buried in the combs while her whole frame twists under the strain. There is always the danger of foundering, something which very rarely happens in tidewater. Vessels that have survived violent storms on the ocean have, in fact, been known to sink under the onslaught of the gales on the Great Lakes.

Obviously then, construction of the new 600 ft. ore carrier aimed towards maximum constructural strength. The keel was constructed of sheet steel, forming a continuous-type girder nearly 600 ft. long and over six ft. wide. Space between outer and inner hulls was divided into small compartments through the utilization of ribs riveted on both sides to the keel. Some of the ribs had holes in them to allow water to enter for use as ballast, while others were solid, to form watertight compartments. Any one of these sections would be filled or emptied at will without regard to the others.

A series of arched girders were placed above the upper ends of uprights and formed supports for the main deck. The hatchways were between them. The ribs, uprights and arches were all linked for added strength, and the plates which covered the frame were made of 3/4″ steel.

Machinery was located in a separate watertight compartment at the stern of the ship. The first ship with hatches spaced on 12 ft. centers, as all ore boats were until the 1930s, was the *James H. Hoit,* launched in 1903.

While the first 600 ft. vessels were built in 1906, it was just two years later, in 1908, that the first *self-unloading carrier* was launched.

The Golden Days of passenger steamer service on the Great Lakes can be seen in these pictures of the steamer United States taken at Saugatuck, Mich., loaded to the gunnells with passengers. The liner being towed by the tug, B.F. Bruce is the Theodore Roosevelt. In winter storage (opposite page) are the North and South America and the Alabama, the former two owned and operated by the Chicago-Duluth and Georgian Bay Transit Company while the United States and Theodore Roosevelt were the property of the Michigan City and Chicago Line.

The first lock at Sault Ste. Marie, with a side-wheeler in transit.

The Canada Steamship Lines vessel Kenora undergoing repairs in 1924 in the Port of Ogdensburg.

The steamer William Livingstone *in the Livingstone Channel, October 1912.*

In 1928 there were 43 self-unloading vessels on the Great Lakes and by 1936 there were 65; fifty-four of these were American registry and 10 Canadian. These vessels handled most types of dry bulk cargo.

Engines for the earlier giant carriers were expansion screw propeller types, developing 2,200 HP and 120 rpm. The cylinders were 24, 39 and 65 inches in diameter. The boilers, each 15 ft. in diameter by 12 ft. long, weighed nearly 100 tons. The normal speed of the 600 ft. young giants was between 10 and 12 mph.

In the early 20th century, as today, U.S. Steel owned the largest single fleet flying the American Flag in any waters in the world. The fleet in the early part of the 20th century consisted of 105 vessels, including 78 steamers and 27 barges and schooners, with a total registry tonnage of 400,000 and a cargo capacity on a single trip basis of 3/4 of a million tons.

During the first decade of the new century, the Detroit River was a mass with ships traveling in each direction, at an average of one every six minutes. There would be *rabbits*,

with cargoes of coal, stone and salt; the *hookers* and their barges of lumber; *schooners* or *lighters* towed by a tug. There would be a *whaleback* and a barge downbound with ore or heading north with coal. Modern *passenger liners* would be there, too, with crowds of passengers at their railings. Then, too, the large *steamers* of the mail and express services would be there, and the giant *car ferries* moving cargoes of five railroad lines.

Into all of this upbound and downbound traffic would steam the *ore ships* of the 400 and 500 ft. class and, with just a little luck, a boat buff might see one of the giant *new 600-footers*.

In a single navigation season, the number of passages during this time at Detroit was nearly 38,000—more than 10 times the reported passages at the Suez Canal. Cargo totals exceeded 67,250,000 tons, far more than that by all ships in all the ports of Great Britain in one year, and also exceeding the total tonnage entering the harbors of New York, Baltimore, Philadelphia, Boston, Charleston and Savannah.

SPECIAL PHOTO SECTION III

Above, a unique and complex vessel, the Detroit Edison. *Below, the self-unloader* Myron C. Taylor, *part of the U.S. Steel fleet.*

A busy loading area with the laker Quebecois *in the foreground and, behind it, U.S. Steel oil carrier George A. Sloan with its conveyor extended for off-loading. Below the hold of a carrier with taconite is loaded by conveyor.*

A Coast Guard icebreaker, lights ablaze, works at night fo free a carrier stuck in the ice. Below, the William P. Snyder of Cleveland Cliffs Iron Co. moves through a channel already broken by the icebreaker.

The Benjamin Fairless *moves in Lake Superior for another load of taconite while a sister ship heads toward the mills with the precious ore. Below, an icebreaker comes to the rescue of a vessel locked in ice.*

The difference between lake freight and the tariffs of the railroads early in the new century represented about $90,000,000 annually.

When World War I came, the United States had virtually no merchant marine, so many shipyards around the Great Lakes joined the shipyards of the tidewater coasts by producing small vessels that could get out of the Lakes via the Welland Canal, to make their way to salt-water and to the war. The ships were small but they were ships, and became known as Welland Canalers.

The vessels, in order to come through the Welland at that time, could be no longer than 261 ft. overall, 43 ft. 6 inches at beam and a depth of 13 ft. With only 1/10th of the total U.S. shipbuilding capacity in the Great Lakes, the Litton yards at Erie built nearly 20% of the total tonnage delivered to the U.S. during the war.

With the advent of peace, the Welland Canalers could not compete in commercial trade because of their size, but many were used in coastal trades, and many others returned to the Great Lakes.

The famous "Poker Fleet" of the Lakes— they had been named *ace, king, queen, jack,* etc.—was comprised mostly of Welland Canalers. Many other Canalers found their way to the blast furnaces while still others cut into barges for Great Lakes operations and carried the name "Lake" as part of their full name.[9]

The development of the railroads in America soon encroached upon the well established traffic in the Great Lakes, as the rails sought their share of trade. The completion of a rail line extending across the northern portion of Ohio, including Cleveland and Toledo, marked the first active competition between the railways and the waterways. The Lake Shore Railroad, connecting with the New York Central, created a line all the way to New York to the east and the west connected southern Michigan and northern Indiana from a continuous line to Chicago.

Although separate and distinct, these railroads exerted tremendous influence on east and west bound cargoes. As if this weren't enough, the Great Western Railway of Canada pushed its rails from the east all the way to Detroit, completing another access from Buffalo to Chicago. Soon traffic patterns were so well established that commerce began to shift from water to land.

Passenger traffic was the first to go, followed soon by cargoes of produce, meat and other perishable foodstuffs. The rails kept going when the ships were stopped by ice. Scheduling was meticulous. Trains departed on time, arrived on time, and were highly professional. Coupled with the problems brought on by the railroads, water transportation also faced a diminishing of immigration into the region, and with the decline, a drastic reduction in both the passenger and cargo commerce it had previously generated.

Water transportation tried to compete by building the larger, faster steamships. But it simply didn't work. By 1857 the Great Lakes fleet had dwindled to an incredible low of just 107 sidewheel steamboats, 135 propeller driven crafts and 1,006 sailing vessels of all classes.

The opening of the Soo Canal and locks in 1855 and the resultant opening of Lake Superior to traffic from the other lakes created some benefit for water transportation. Now traffic could travel, albeit with low drafts, from the St. Lawrence River to the Lakehead. The opening of the Soo actually sounded the beginning of what was to become a very important era in Great Lakes commerce — the movement of iron and copper ore from the upper lakes to the mills of the south. This is the moment that lead to the birth of the modern-day lake carrier—the giant ore boats of the Great Lakes fleet.

[9]When World War II broke out, Welland Canalers that remained were taken over once again by the Federal government and hurried into war service.

The Great Lakes ice blockade of 1926 saw 150 ships frozen in below the locks at the Soo. The Chief Wawatam *brought from Mackinac along with five tugs, worked for three weeks to release the vessels. They succeeded in breaking out all but 26 carriers, and these remained at the Soo all winter long.*

Lake steamers are shown unloading grain at elevators in Buffalo. The early grain elevators and Erie Canal barges were typical to the waterfront activity in this era at Buffalo when that port city was an important transfer point between the Great Lakes and the Erie Barge Canal.

The steamer Lake Ledan *was built at Superior in 1918 for the Cunard Steamship Company, famous for the Liners* Queen Mary *and* Queen Elizabeth. *She was one of a number of small ocean-going ships that were built in the Great Lakes. Only a handful of ships were delivered before the United States entered the First World War, and those under construction were requisitioned by the government, which contracted to build more than 400 additional ships of similar design. This vessel was built by the Superior Shipbuilding Company to a length of 261 feet and a beam of 43 feet. Numerous other shipyards joined the emergency shipbuilding program and most of the vessels commissioned were given the prefix name,* Lake. *Camouflage design was carefully painted to government specifications, with less than an inch tolerance for error. There is hardly a port in the world that has not been visited by a* Lake *ocean ship at one time or another. Some of the vessels actually returned to their native Great Lakes, including the* Lake Ledan *which worked for the Ford Motor Company until 1927. Others returning to the Lakes include the famous* Poker Fleet, *bearing the names* Ace, Queen, King, Jack *and* Ten.

Sailing out of Toronto in 1955 is the Fernie, *a Canada Steamship vessel.*

4

The Great Shipping Companies

The turn of the century saw virtually an end to individual ship owners as a dominant force in lake transportation. Now rose the great shipping companies—the giant firms which built and operated vessels to meet their own needs, and in so doing, created the large fleets which are active in the Great Lakes today. Not the least of these were the railroads.

In the early decades of the century, on Lake Ontario and the upper portion of the St. Lawrence, commercial traffic was almost entirely Canadian. Large ocean and coastal vessels traveled from the Gulf of St. Lawrence to Montreal, bringing in cargo for Canada and returning to Europe with grain and general cargo. It is not surprising, therefore, that commerce in the eastern-most of the Lakes should be carried on Canadian bottoms. At the time, the dominant force in water commerce was growing out of the Richelieu and Ontario Navigation Company.

It was also the oldest transport line in Canada, emerging from origins which began with a small company known as *Le Société Navigation Du Richelieu*, owned by farmers from the Richelieu river valley. The company was formed to run boats which carried the products of the farms in the valley to the markets at Montreal. The service proved to be so important that the line was eventually extended to include towns along the St. Lawrence River.

The fleet started with one steamboat, the *Jacques Cartier*, and one barge. By 1856 two steamers were added, the *Napoleon* and *Vic-*

toria, and in 1875 the Richelieu Company merged with the Canadian Navigation Company and the Union Navigation Company and the name change took place. Larger and more modern vessels were added until it became the largest in Canadian commerce.

By 1880 four other navigation companies were brought under Richelieu and Ontario management. The fleet, at the beginning of the century, consisted of 26 steamers which, in themselves, represent the evolution of Canadian commerce in shipbuilding from 1847 until the First World War.

Richelieu and Ontario came to a United States shipyard in 1909 for the construction of a vessel to enter the coastal trade of the southern shore of Lake Ontario and the St. Lawrence River. Their fleet could not serve this trade because of maritime laws which barred foreign-built ships from trading between ports of the United States. Foreign vessels could trade between foreign ports and U.S. ports, and *vice versa*, but they could not handle shipments of cargo from one U.S. port to another. The steamer *Rochester*, therefore, in 1910, established a new route for the company as it plied between the Niagara River, Rochester, Oswego and the Thousand Islands.

The largest fleet operating in the U.S. at this time was popularly known as the Steel Trust Fleet. It was owned and operated by the Pittsburgh Steamship Company of Cleveland, and it was originally known as the Bessemer Steamship Company. Beginning its career in 1896 with 21 vessels, the line grew to a fleet of

The Shenango *fleet is pictured handsomely in this undated photo.*

78 steamships and 16 barges in the 1830s, becoming a behemoth engaged in the transport of iron and coal and, at the close of the 19th century, became known as the mighty U.S. Steel Great Lakes Fleet, the largest on the Lakes.

Besides these two giants, there were some 40 or 50 other companies engaged in the same class of traffic in the early decades of the century. The Goodrich Line of Chicago, for instance, established in 1856, included among its registry the *S.S. Christopher Columbus*, the only whaleback ever built for passenger service. The G.A. Tomlinson fleet of Cleveland represented the largest group of ships controlled by one man and included the Continental Steamship Co., The Duluth Steamship Co., Globe Steamship Co., Inter-Ocean Steamship Co., National Steamship Co., Panda Steamship Co., Trinton Steamship Co. and Zenith Steamship Co.

Other U.S. lines included: the Cleveland and Buffalo Lines, Cleveland-Cliffs Iron Co., Chicago; Duluth and Georgian Bay Transit Co.; Michigan Transportation Co.; Columbia Steamship Co.; Pickands Mather and Co.; Oglebay-Norton and Co.; Great Lakes Steamship Co.; Hutchinson and Co.; Pioneer Steamship Co. (Boland & Cornelius) and the Geo. Hall Co., among others.

On the Canadian side was the Canada Pacific Co., Federal Commerce and Navigation, Keystone Transports, Ltd., Sarnia Steamships, Ltd., Patterson Steamship, Ltd., Eastern Steamship Co., Ltd., Three Line Navigation Co., and many others.

In the 1920s there were about 350 U.S. and Canadian shipping companies operating vessels on the Great Lakes, numbering close to 2,000 vessels.

Mergers and acquisitions played a major role in the development of many of the giant lines operating in the Lakes today. An example of this maritime development can be seen in the structure of one company:

A Lake Ontario company known as the Royal Mail Line of Niagara and Toronto merged with Richelieu and Ontario in 1913 and the firm continued with a new and now famous name: Canada Steamship Line. The merger brought together many famous shipping companies, including the Montreal Transportation Co., the Northern Navigation Co., the Niagara Navigation Co., the Hamilton Steamship Co. and Turbin Steamship Co.—all of which operated day excursion

The Lakeshell *proudly displays her Shell Oil Company banner. Loading and unloading tankers was a pretty primitive job then, as is illustrated by the photo below.*

steamers with freight accommodations on Lake Ontario.

Freight lines included by merger were the Inland Line, Merchants Mutual Lines, Merchants Montreal Lines, Midland Navigation Co. and Playfair Steamship Co.

Also operating in the interlake commerce of Canada at this time with a number of large vessels was the St. Lawrence and Chicago Steam Navigation Co., the Montreal Transportation Co., the Merchant-Montreal Line and the Canada-Atlantic Transportation Co. All of these lines operated on the Lake Ontario-St. Lawrence River region, while on the upper lakes water commerce was moved by several other lines, the largest of which was the Northern Navigation Co., a division of the Grand Trunk System. Northern Navigation controlled most of the passenger and freight service between Western Ontario and the head of Lake Superior.

In 1901, U.S. Steel fixed a rate of 80¢ a ton on the transportation of its ore to the furnaces. A ton was "2,240 pounds." This established the rate at which all other carriers worked. The vessel owner paid 19¢ per ton dockage and unloading charges at lower lake ports.

The cost of running a ship then was between $500 and $800 a day.

At the turn of the century, the coal rate from Lake Erie ports to the upper lakes ranged between 25 and 50¢ a ton in the summer and

The busy Straits of Mackinac.

The opening of the Sabin Lock at the St. Marys Falls Canal on September 18, 1919.

70

in December, when hardy vessels made last-minute runs through the incredible November storms, the rate soared to as high as $1.00 a ton.

Under these conditions, a 600 ft. ore carrier coming down in late November with a full cargo of 400,000 bushels of wheat, could collect a freight bill of about $12,000. It could then load with 13,000 tons of coal and twenty-four hours later, could be heading for a western port. By the close of the year—a couple of days later—she would arrive in Chicago or Milwaukee with another $15,000 worth of cargo or $25,000 for the round trip, all earned in about 10 days.

For the decade 1926-1935, the average annual tonnage of the combined Great Lakes ports was 114.8 million short tons. Nearly half of that total was handled at six ports: Superior (with an average of 38 million tons, largely iron ore), Toledo (an average of 17.2 million tons also largely iron ore), Buffalo (17.1 million tons, including New York Barge Canal traffic), Chicago (12 million tons), Cleveland (10.8 million tons, also largely iron ore), and Ashtabula (8.8 million tons, also largely iron ore).

For that ten year period, Lake Erie was accountable for 40% of the tonnage, with Lake Superior with 25%, Lake Michigan with 22%, Lake Huron 5% and Lake Ontario less than 1%.

The Robert W.E. Bunsen *of the Pittsburgh Steamship Company, Marine City, Michigan, moves up-river near an old sailing vessel, the* J.T. Wing, *a grain boat.*

A 1938 Listing of U.S. Great Lakes Ore Boat Fleets

Fleet	Number of Ships	Capacity Per Trip	Average Size
Pittsburgh Steamship Company	79	715,400	9,056
Interlake Steamship Company	45	397,200	8,827
Hutchinson & Co., Managers	22	190,500	8,659
Cleveland Cliffs Iron Company	24	185,300	7,721
Bethlehem Transportation Company	16	159,400	9,963
Great Lakes Steamship Company	19	144,300	7,595
Wilson Transit Company	13	111,600	8,585
Columbia Transportation Company	14	107,200	7,657
The M. A. Hanna Co., Agents	11	104,500	9,500
G. A. Tomlinson	10	85,400	8,540
Reiss Steamship Company	10	80,900	8,090
Boland & Cornelius	8	62,200	7,775
Buckeye Steamship Company	11	59,000	5,364
Midland Steamship Company	7	54,600	7,800
Interstate Steamship Company	4	40,600	10,150
H. & G. M. Steinbrenner	4	35,500	8,875
Shenango Steamship Company	3	34,400	11,467
Ford Motor Company	2	21,800	10,900
Wisconsin Steel Company	2	20,800	10,400
D. Sullivan & Company	2	15,600	7,800
Brown & Company	2	14,000	7,000
	308	2,640,200	8,572

A self-unloading bulk carrier, the Ocean Trade.

A rough sea.

Washing down the decks on a choppy sea.

The Welland Ship Canal in 1950, looking north from the west entrance wall of Lock No. 1.

The Edmund Fitzgerald.

5

When Disaster Strikes

The sinking of any ship is always a frightening and dramatic event. Man somehow sees a vessel as a living thing, assigning to it both a personality and a personal pronoun—*her*. The loss of life couples, somehow, with the loss of this personality of a ship, this anthropomorphic identification, to send a shock wave around the world whenever the sinking of a major vessel occurs.

This is all the more true in a geographically confined maritime community such as the Great Lakes, where vessels and crew members are known throughout the system. This close relationship became vividly apparent in the November 1975 loss of the *Edmund Fitzgerald*.

On November 11 of that year, Oglebay Norton Company of Cleveland put out a terse release which said, "The steamer *Edmund Fitzgerald* was reported missing during severe weather near Whitefish Point in Lake Superior, on the evening of Monday, November 10. The Coast Guard reported at noon on November 11th that the vessel was still missing and presumed lost. Search and rescue operations for the vessel, which began Monday evening, are continuing under the direction of the Coast Guard."

The steamer *Fitzgerald* departed the Duluth-Superior harbor at 2:50 p.m. on November 9th, after loading a cargo of 26,116 gross tons of taconite pellets bound for Detroit. The vessel routinely reported her position on Lake Superior on the morning of November 10th.

The *Fitzgerald*, designed for Great Lakes-St. Lawrence River operations, was commissioned in 1958 at Great Lakes Engineering Works, River Rouge, Mich. The vessel had a cargo capacity of 27,500 gross tons, an overall length of 729 ft. and was driven by a steam-driven engine rated at 7,500 HP. She carried a crew of 29.

The *Fitzgerald* was actually owned by the Northwestern Mutual Life Insurance Company of Milwaukee and was a long-term charter of the Columbia Transportation Division of Oglebay Norton.

When Oglebay Norton released the names and home towns of the 29 crew members, typically, and with only two exceptions, all of the men were from states which border the Great Lakes.

A $150,000 Coast Guard inquiry into the sinking of the *Fitzgerald* brought into the Great Lakes highly sophisticated U.S. Navy underwater closed-circuit TV cameras, which quickly identified and pictured the wrecked freighter near the entrance to Whitefish Bay.

A 15 ft. underwater sled carrying the two closed-circuit TV cameras and a still camera were used in the operation. The sled, known as CURV III, was developed by the Naval Undersea Research and Development Center. (The predecessor to CURV III had been used to recover a hydrogen bomb off Spain in 1966.

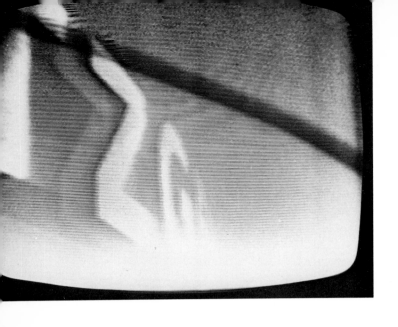

The letters 'T . . . Z . . . G . . .' as seen by underwater camera on the stern section of the Edmund Fitzgerald, where she lies 350 feet below Lake Superior is mute evidence to the wreckage of the 729 foot carrier. Below, Coast Guard and Navy personnel load CURV III equipment aboard the Coast Guard cutter Woodrush for the discovery operation. (See text)

The present machine can take 500 photographs without reloading and can video-tape indefinitely.)

TV monitors aboard the Coast Guard cutter *Woodrush* showed the stern section of the vessel upside down in 530 ft. of water. It showed the bow right side up.

The carrier was first located on November 11, identified by a tell-tale oil slick. She was then more precisely located by Navy aircraft which used a magnetic detection device. Side-scan sonar was then used to show that the *Fitzgerald* had broken into three sections.

The 729 ft. *Fitzgerald*, if stood on end, the Coast Guard has indicated, would protrude a towering 200 feet above the surface of the Lake Superior waters in which she had sunk. Yet, at the bottom, "she might as well be on the moon for all we are able to find out," noted Captain James A. Wilson of the Coast Guard at Detroit.

There is some indication that the *Fitzgerald* had passed close to the shallows of Caribou Island, leading to the speculation that she might have scraped bottom at that point. Other investigations consider the fact that the vessel, with over 26,000 tons of taconite pellets aboard, might have run into clay bottom while moving at 30 m.p.h.

Accidents are virtually unheard of at the Soo Locks, but a bad one occurred in 1909 in the Canadian locks, when a Canadian Pacific passenger steamer entered the Locks and waited to be lowered the 20 ft.-plus drop to the Lake Huron level. A freighter, the *Crescent City*, entered the upper gates to lock down with the steamer. On the other side, waiting to be locked up to Lake Superior, was a bulk freighter, the *Perry G. Walker*.

The skipper of the *Crescent City* gave the signal to stop and reverse engines, but instead, for some unknown reason, the vessel moved forward at full speed, colliding with the lower gates and tearing them loose from their moorings.

With the upper lock gates not yet closed, a wall of water 20 feet high crashed through the locks and out of the open and broken lower gates. The CP passenger ship, torn from her lines, fell forward with the onslaught of water,

These dramatic pictures were taken at Sault Ste. Marie after a down-bound vessel crashed through the lower lock gates, sending a 12-foot wall of water cascading into the lower reaches of the St. Marys River, tossing ore and passenger boats about like toy boats (See text).

hit the *Perry G. Walker* and forced her onto the shoals of the channel, grounding her.

The *Crescent City*, loaded with heavy ore, was trapped in the cascading waters and was swept through the locks, tearing a hole in her side, striking the CP vessel as she plummeted downstream. When the melee ended, tugs from the United States were rushed to the scene, restored order and brought the ships under control.

Damage to the docks ran over a quarter of a million dollars and over $100,000 to the *Cres-*

cent City. The damage to the other two vessels was slight, although the shock and the indignities were great, and made legends out of both vessels.

Many excellent volumes have been written about the historic shipwrecks of the Great Lakes, and while a mention of a few of the most noteworthy carrier sinkings probably belongs in this volume, the interested reader is referred to more specific books devoted entirely to wrecks, sinkings and marine disasters of the Lakes. [10]

Probably the best known of the old-time sinkings was that of the steamer *Pewabic,* which sank in Lake Huron four months following the close of the Civil War, carrying a cargo of copper. A propeller-driven vessel, the *Pewabic* was struck by a cruise ship, the *Meteor.* A hole was cut above and below her water line and within ten minutes she sank in 180 ft. of water. Some 125 persons died from

the two vessels. The *Meteor* was eventually repaired and put to work in Great Lakes commerce, where she worked until World War I, when she was cut into a tow barge and her name changed to the *Nelson Boom.*

The second worst tragedy in the Great Lakes was a collision between a passenger steamer, the *Lady Elgin,* and a freight schooner. On September 8, 1860 on Lake Michigan, the 300 ft. paddle-wheeler was carrying 400 passengers to Milwaukee.

A tremendous impact split open the port side of the *Lady Elgin* as the loaded schooner, *Augusta* cut into her below the water line. The schooner continued on without stopping.

Some 297 persons lost their lives. At that time in the maritime history of the Lakes, the law permitted freighters to operate without lights, making it the responsibility of luxury vessels to keep out of their way. So, the captain of the schooner was not blamed for the sinking.

[10]*Seaway,* by Jacques LesStrang, published 1976 by Superior Publishing Co., the companion volume to *The Lake Carriers,* also contains photographs and text on modern-day Great Lakes sinkings.

Below, a boom is deployed by the Coast Guard in an effort to assist commercial firms with oil spill clean-up operations.

An icebreaker view of a rescue operation (top). Below, the Ojibway, work boat of the U.S. Steel fleet, brings supplies through the ice to the winter navigating vessels.

A cold day at sea (top).
Carrier moves along a track cut by a Coast Guard
vessel barely visible on the horizon.

On a beach strewn with logs and debris are the beached three masted vessels the Moonlight and the Kent.

The storm of November 30, 1905 has been called one of the most violent to ever hit Lake Superior. It was, most agreed, the most destructive storm since the days of the steel ships and the bulk freight trade. So intense was the weather that the steamer *John Stanton*, bound for Fort Williams with a cargo of coal, worked her engine at full speed, continuously for 14 hours and during all that time, simply moved astern. The steamer *Crescent City*, (which we have already met) released both anchors and with her engines wide open for nearly four hours, went helplessly with the storm and ended up on the rocks at Duluth.

Vessels that were lost or damaged in the storm include the steamers *Mataafa*, *Lafayette*, *Edinborn*, *Coralis*, *William E. Corey*, *Crescent City*, *Isaac L. Ellwood*, *England*, *Western Star*, *Bransford*, *Monkshaven*, *George Spencer*, *Ambov*, *Ira H. Owen*, *Veg*, *D.C. Whitney*, *C.H. Warner*, *Ferdinand Schlesigner*, *Rosemont*, *J.H. Outhwaite*, plus schooners *Vinland* and *Georgia* and barges *Manilla*, *Maderia* and *Maia*.

Many books have been written about the storm of 1913. Statistics vary on the loss of lives and ships, but estimates talk of 35 ships that either went down or were washed ashore and a loss of life near 250. The storm occurred between November 7 and 11.

The Lake Carrier's Association, after the storm, reported that no lake master could recall a storm of such unprecedented violence or with such rapid changes in the direction of the wind.

Storms of that intensity on the Lakes don't last over four or five hours, the Association

The pilot house of the Harriet B. *was photographed in 1922 at Knife River, Minnesota on Lake Superior, after it floated ashore following the sinking of the vessel. The* Harriet B. *collided in a heavy fog with the freighter,* Quincy A. Shaw.

reported, but the storm of November 1913 raged for 16 hours, with an average velocity of 60 m.p.h. and frequent spurts of 70 and over.

"Testimony of (ship) masters," the Association reported at the time, "report waves at least 35 ft. high following each other in quick succession. Being at such heights and heralded at such force and such rapid succession, the ships must have been subjected to incredible punishment.

"Masters also relate that the wind and sea were frequently in conflict, the wind blowing one way and the sea running in the opposite direction, indicating a storm of cyclonic nature. It may be centuries before such a combination of forces may be experienced again."

In the port cities surrounding the lakes, land traffic was virtually paralyzed, as were communications and power lines.

Newspapers carried long lists of boats hit by the gale and one such list indicated the following:

"The storm . . . accounted for the greatest losses in the history of inland navigation . . . 19 vessels were totally destroyed; 20 stranded. Of those destroyed, 10 were lost in Lake Huron, three in Lake Michigan, one in Lake Erie and five in Lake Superior. Of those stranded, six were in Lake Huron, three in Lake Erie, five in Lake Superior, one in Georgian Bay, one on the St. Marys River, one at Simmon's Reef, Straits of Mackinaw, one at the Livingston Channel of the Detroit River and two in St. Clair."

The value of vessels and cargo lost combined to $10.3 million. Of this total, $5.2 million was lost on Lake Huron. Lives lost totalled 248.

"Eight ships disappeared with all on board," the newspaper report concluded, "and nothing was ever heard from them except for on the *Charles S. Price* which turned upside down and remained that way until she sank."

The ships that were lost include: *Argus*, Lake Huron, 25 lost; *James Carruthers*, Lake Huron, 22 lost; *Hydrus*, Lake Huron, 25 lost; *Leafield*, Lake Superior, 18 lost; *John A. McGean*, Lake Huron, 23 lost; *Charles S. Price*, Lake Huron, 28 lost; *Regina*, Lake Huron, 28 lost; *Isaac M. Scott*, Lake Huron, 28 lost; *Henry B. Smith*, Lake Superior, 25 lost; *Wexford*, Lake Huron, 24 lost; *Lightship No. 82*, Lake Erie, 6 lost.

Others that were wrecked in the storm included: *William Nottingham*, ashore in Whitefish Bay, 3 lost; *Howard M. Hanna*, ashore in Lake Huron, no lives lost, *L.C. Waldo*, ashore on Manitou Island, Lake Superior, no lives lost; *Lightship No. 61*, blown ashore at head of St. Clair River; *John T. Hutchinson*, ashore at Point Iroquois in Lake Superior; *Northern Queen*, ashore near Kettle Point in Lake Huron, crew rescued; *Plymouth*, difficulty at Harbor Beach, Mich., vessel released herself; *H.B. Hagwood*, ashore at Corsica Shoal, lower end of Lake Huron, no lives lost.

Hardwick, aground near Port Huron, Mich.; *Saxona*, aground in the St. Clair River, released herself; *Victory*, aground in Livingstone Channel near Detroit, lightened cargo and was released; *Thistle*, ashore at Calumet Harbor, Mich.; *G.J. Grammer*, beached one half mile east of harbor entrance at Lorain Ohio, crew rescued.

Halstead, aground near Green Bay, Wis., crew of six missing; *Louisiana*, sunk off Washington Island in Lake Michigan, crew of 15 saved; *Huronic*, aground off Whitefish Point, crew and passengers safe; *Turret Chief*, driven ashore near Copper Harbor, Mich., crew rescued; *Matthew Andrews*, aground on Corsica Shoal, lower Lake Huron.

Interest on the part of news media in oil spills has risen dramatically in recent years because of the national interest in environmental protection. Here a Coast Guard official, Capt. Frederick H. Raumer, Captain of the Port of Detroit and Officer in charge of an oil spill in Michigan's Saginaw River, discusses clean up operations for the TV cameras.

Matoa, ashore near Pt. Aux Barques, Lake Huron; *J.M. Jenks,* ashore in Georgian Bay; *A.E. Stewart,* aground in Whitefish Bay; *F.G. Hartwell,* difficulty in Whitefish Bay, crew taken off; *Acadian,* aground on reef near Sulphur Island in Lake Superior.

Friday, October 20, 1916, still known as "Black Friday" in the Great Lakes, was another day of infamy. In a storm on Lake Erie, four vessels were lost: the Canadian steamer *Merida,* with 20 men aboard; the schooner *D.L. Filer,* one of the last of the Great Lakes sailing fleet, carrying seven men; the *Marshall F.Buters,* a wooden lumber carrier (the crew was saved here); and the *James B. Colgate,* with all hands lost, except one.

On Armistice Day, 1940, another violent storm of note reaped havoc on the Great Lakes. Attacking Lake Michigan, the storm ravaged the *Novadoc,* the *William B. Dovack* and the *Anna C. Mitch,* sinking all three, with all hands on board. The *Novadoc* was a 420 ft. carrier, while the *Mitch,* of Canadian registry, was 380 ft. Both had passed through the Straits of Mackinac into Lake Michigan, coming in contact apparently with the center of the storm.

When the storm abated, half of the *Anna C. Mitch*—the forward half minus the pilot house and forward cabins—was located in 40 ft. of water some 400 ft. from Pentwater Pier. Damage to the port side of the vessel lead experts at the time to believe that the *Mitch* had been hit by the *William B. Dovack* and that both vessels had sunk during the storm. The fact that wreckage and bodies from both ships were washed ashore together helped substantiate that conclusion.

The 1940 Armistice Day storm created wind velocities up to 125 m.p.h. at Lansing Shoal in northern Lake Michigan.

The *A.J. Peterson,* a 253 ft. ocean freighter, was wrecked at St. Helena near the Straits of

A Coast Guard buoy tender Acacia stands by near the overturned Sidney E. Smith at Port Huron, Michigan, in the St. Clair River. Opposite page, divers emerge from the Smith in an effort to remove fuel from her sinking hull in order to avoid environmental damage. The carrier sank in 35 feet of water after collision with a grain carrier. Some 49 thousand gallons of heavy bunker C fuel were ultimately removed from the vessel, which hung precariously off an underwater shelf. The three foot crack in the vessel just forward of mid-ships can be seen in the photo top, left.

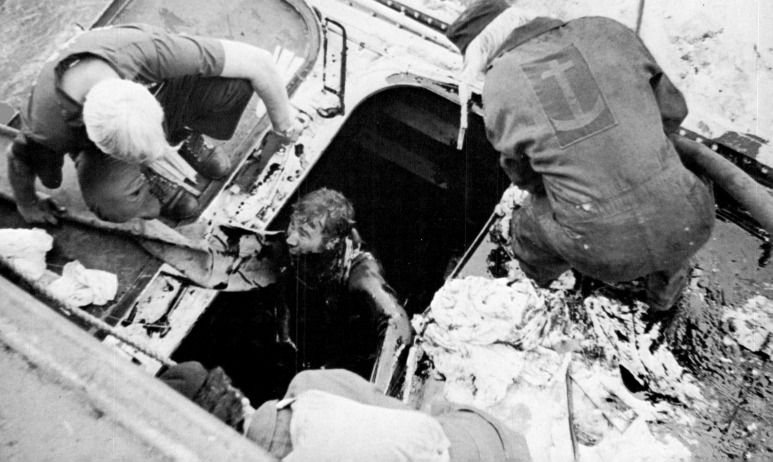

Mackinac. The 416 ft. *Sinoloa*, a gravel carrier, *Conneaut* was washed ashore. Near South Haven, Mich. two large fishing tugs, the *Indian* and the *Richard H.*, were lost.

In Lake Superior, the 305 ft. freighter, the *Sparta* was washed ashore. The list of casualties went on: 392 ft. car ferry, *Flint* was grounded; the package freighter, *Alfred H. Smith* and the tanker *New Haven Socony*, were both damaged, but safe, as were the *Justin C. Allen, Crudoil, Arthur Ore, Empire State, Mercury, Irene* and many, many others.

A year previous, on July 24, an appalling sinking occurred that was publicized worldwide. An overloaded passenger liner, the *Eastland*, rolled over at a pier in Chicago with a loss if 835 lives. The *Eastland*, with 2,500 passengers had been chartered for an excursion to Michigan City, Indiana. As the ship moved slowly from the pier, it gently began to roll from side to side. Passengers laughed. Then the rolling became uncontrollable. As the rocking momentum increased, water rushed through portholes and across the decks. In one final roll, the *Eastland* keeled over on her side. Although she was in only 19 ft. of water, passengers below decks and in cabins never had a chance.

If, on a map of eastern Lake Superior, we draw a line from Grand Marais, Mich., east past Whitefish Point as far as Point Iroquois, then another line NNE past Gros Cap, Goulais Bay and Copper-Mine Point to Cape Gargantua, then westward to Caribou Island and finally southward back to Grand Marais, we have constructed a four sided figure, something less than 100 miles on a side.

Within this trapezium late in the 19th and early 20th century nearly a dozen vessels disappeared due to causes unknown. This number does not include known losses through collision, stranding, fire or other causes. While the Great Lakes might not have anything as baffling as a Bermuda Triangle, its own Whitefish Trapezium has proved to be just as mysteriously disasterous to these early Great Lakes vessels.

Western Reserve, steel bulk freighter, owned by the Minch interests of Cleveland. Built by Cleveland Shipbuilding Co. in 1890, 300 x 41 x 25. Broke up and foundered some 60 miles west of Whitefish Point, Aug. 30, 1892. One survivor, thirty-one lost.

Bannockburn, steel canaler, owned by Montreal Transportation Co. Built by Sir Raylton Dixon & Co., Middlesborough, England in 1893. 244 x 40 x 18. Sailed from Port Arthur, downbound, Nov. 21, 1902 and was never heard from again. One piece of wreckage found near Grand Marais.

Cyprus, steel bulk freighter operated by Pickands Mather for Lackawanna Steamship Co. Built, 1907 at Lorain by American Shipbuilding Co. 420 x 52 x 29. Foundered on downbound leg of second trip, off Deer Park L.S. Station, Oct. 11, 1907. One survivor, who stated that vessel capsized due to water in hold and shifting cargo.

D. M. Clemson, steel bulk freighter operated by Wolvin for Provident Steamship Co. Built by Superior Shipbuilding Co., at Superior, 1903. 448 x 52 x 28. Foundered, upbound, somewhere west of Whitefish Point. Dec. 2, 1908. No survivors, 24 lost.

Henry B. Smith, steel bulk freighter operated by Hawgood for the Acme Transit Co. Built at Lorain in 1906 by American Shipbuilding Co. 525 x 55 x 31. Sailed from Marquette with ore, downbound and was never heard from again following the great storm of Nov. 11, 1913.

C.F. Curtis, wooden steam barge, and consorts *Annie M. Peterson* & *Selden E. Marvin*, sailed from Baraga, Mich. on the Keweenaw Peninsula for the lower lakes, Nov. 18, 1914, loaded with lumber. They were never seen again. Wreckage and bodies came ashore near Grand Marais. (*C.F. Curtis*, 1882 Marine City by Lester. 196 x 32 x 13. *Annie M. Peterson*, 1874 Green Bay, Wis. 190 x 33 x 13. *Selden E. Marvin*, 1881 Toledo, 175 x 33 x 12. All three belonged to Edward Hines Lumber Co., Chicago.)

Cerisoles and *Inkerman*, steel trawler-type minesweepers, built by Canadian Car & Foundry Co., Fort William for the French Navy. 136 x 26 x 13. Sailed together from Fort William for Sault Ste. Marie and were never heard from again. Exact location of loss is not known, as no wreckage was found and no bodies recovered. Seventy-six lives were lost from the two ships.

The recovery of cargoes from wrecks and from sunken ships is an integral part of the Great Lakes maritime picture, of course, and the fleet that salvage companies maintain is indeed unique. They include large sea-going tugs, strong vessels able to stand virtually any sea, equipped with engines capable of towing, pumping or lifting, and a crew of expert divers. There are also floats, fitted with cranes with straight lifting power, lighters to take off the vessel's cargo if necessary, and barges to carry the material back to shore.

The grandest of all the wrecking vessels on the Lakes in the early 20th century was the steamer *Favorite* owned by the Great Lakes Towing Co. She was virtually unsinkable. Below her decks were to be found just about every machine or tool devised by man for the destruction of ships.

The vessel was a veritable floating machine shop and forge. Large punches, shears, drill presses, lathes, forges, air drills, pneumatic riveting and tripping hammers, and fire pumps were efficiently located, along with arc lights, to be placed above wrecks.

The *Favorite's* towing equipment contained 1,800 ft. of cable 2″ thick, located forward on coal bunkers and a three drum hoisting engine worked in conjunction with a clam shell bucket with a capacity of 25 tons. The grab or bucket could lift 3 tons of ore, coal or grain in one sweep. There were also jacks weighing 650 pounds each, 30-100 ton jacks, 1,060 ton jacks, air compressors, along with great quantities of suction and rotary equipment.

The Port Huron Wrecking Co. with the wrecker *Charles Diefenbach* was another well-known wrecking company at the turn of the century, as were the Reid Wrecking Co. and Midland Tow and Wrecking Co.

When a ship was submerged in not more than 25 ft. of water, the best way to get at it was to build a *coffer dam* upon and around the vessel, or a good portion of it. This water-tight wall of wood and sheet piling held back the water around the vessel so salvage crews could work on it. When holes in the vessel's hull were patched and the vessel was pumped out, it would rise and could then be towed to a drydock for repairs.

Often damage to a ships' bottom precluded patching the hull. (This kind of damage could result from a cracking of plates on a reef or shoal.) In this case, as much cargo as possible would be removed. Hatches would be sealed tight and decks would be strengthened with cross beams. Then compressed air would be pumped into the vessel, gradually forcing out the water inside the hold. With the cushion of air inside, the vessel would rise enough to be towed to drydock. Pontoons are also used for salvage.

Ships driven on reefs or rocky shoals, especially in Lake Superior, are seldom if ever saved because they are soon battered to pieces long before salvage vessels can reach them.

Lying in 12 ft. of water forward and 90 ft. at stern, the steamer Western Star *is salvaged by Cleveland's Great Lakes Towing Co. The 416-ft. vessel is under about 60 ft. of water at stern. Wrecked on September 24, 1915 on Robertson Rock, Clapperton Island, Georgian Bay in Lake Huron, she sank with a load of 7,000 tons of coal. The coffer dam which Great Lakes Towing used in the recovery operation is 60 ft. high at stern.*

A busy Seaway lock.

6

The Physical Plant: Seaway to the Sault

The Great Lakes are a maritime miracle. There's really no other way to think of it. Here, in the center of a continent, lie five lakes of immense proportions—an eighth sea—rising 600 feet from heartland to tidewater, and connected to the Atlantic Ocean by raging rapids and towering waterfalls. The conquest of these natural obstacles through the man-made miracle of locks and dams and channels led to the establishment of ports and harbors which, once properly fitted out, created the matrix upon which one of the greatest maritime fleets in the world was born, and has flourished.

The Lakes Themselves

The Lakes lie between latitude *41°21' and 49°00' N* and longitude *76°04' and 92°06' W*. Lake Superior, the most northerly and westerly of the group, extends from west to east for 383 miles and from north to south for 160 miles. Lake Michigan extends for 321 miles from north to south and 118 miles from east to west, and Lake Huron from northwest to southwest for 247 miles and east to west for 241 miles and north to south for 57 miles. Lake Erie extends 240 miles northeast and 57 miles south. The fifth lake, Ontario, extends from east to west for 193 miles and from north to south for 53 miles. In all, there are 7,870 miles of shoreline and 95,170 square miles water surface in the Lakes—60,960 in the United States and 34,210 in Canada.

Free of lunar tides and with only light surface currents, the Lakes, in forming the northeastern boundary between the United States and Canada, are the site of two of the largest U.S. cities, with populations in excess of 1,000,000—Chicago and Detroit—and two of the largest cities in Canada—Toronto and Montreal.

Briefly looking at each lake, we find that Ontario is the smallest and the most easterly of the Lakes. Bounded on the north by the Province of Ontario and on the south by the state of New York, it was named by the Iroquois Indians.

Lake Huron, by contrast, is the second largest lake. Bordered on the west by Michigan, and on the north and east by Ontario, it is appended by Georgian Bay on the east. Nearly 580 ft. above sea level, Huron covers 23,000 square miles and its greatest depth is 570 ft. It is fed from Lake Superior via the St. Marys River, from Lake Michigan and numerous streams.

Lake Erie, second from the smallest of the Lakes, borders the states of Michigan, Ohio, Pennsylvania, New York and the Province of Ontario. The shallowest of the Great Lakes, too, it is 570 ft. in average altitude and has a surface area of 9,930 square miles. Its maximum depth is 210 ft., with an average depth of 58 ft. The Lake has a water volume of 109 cubic miles, a little more than one thirtieth that of Lake Superior.

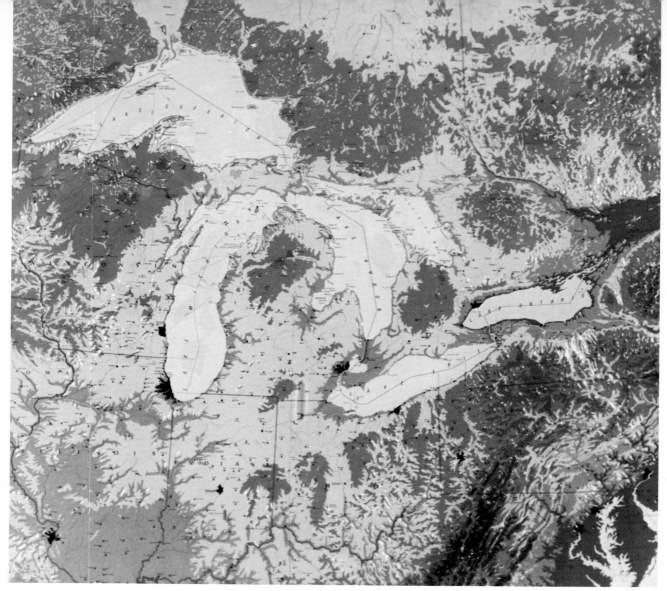

The Great Lakes.

Superior, the most northwesterly of the five Great Lakes, is the largest single body of fresh water in the world. Bounded on the east and north by Ontario, and on the west and south by Minnesota, Wisconsin and Michigan, the lake is fed by nearly 200 rivers.

Superior discharges 68,000 cubic ft. of water per second at its mouth at St. Marys River. This figure is increased to 225,000 cubic ft. per second when these waters are merged with those of Lake Michigan, Lake Huron and Georgian Bay. Following this immense structure of water through Lake Erie, the watershed increases the total 265,000 cubic ft. at Niagara, and rises to 300,000 as

the St. Lawrence River picks up the rushing waters and carries them onward to the sea.

Lake Michigan is the third largest of the Great Lakes and the only one located entirely within the boundaries of the United States. It is bordered on the east and north by Michigan, and on the west and southwest by Wisconsin, Illinois and Indiana. It connects with Lake Huron at the Straits of Mackinac. Lake Michigan is 579 ft. above mean sea level, and covers 22,400 square miles. Its greatest depth is 923 ft.

Three systems of locks exist in the Great Lakes—really in the constructed channels which connect lake-to-lake or lake-to-sea.

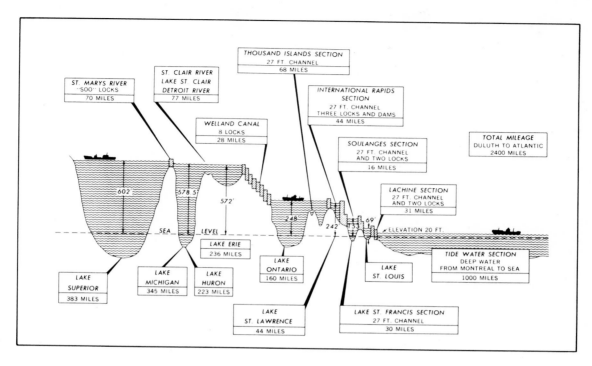

Profile of the Great Lakes-St. Lawrence Seaway system.

The Great Lakes Area

	Water Surface Square Miles	Watershed Square Miles
Lake Superior	31,200	51,600
St. Marys River	150	800
Lake Michigan	22,450	37,700
Lake Huron and Georgian Bay	23,800	31,700
St. Clair River	25	3,800
Lake St. Clair	410	3,400
Detroit River	25	1,200
Lake Erie	9,960	22,700
Niagara River	15	300
Lake Ontario	7,240	21,600

Total area of drainage basin—270,075.

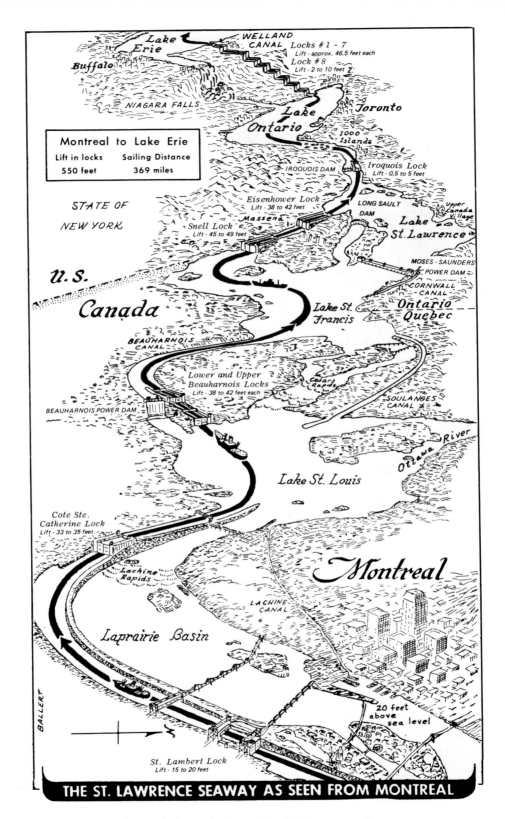

An artist's rendering of the St. Lawrence Seaway as
seen from Montreal. (Dr. Albert G. Ballert)

One is the lock system at Sault Ste. Marie where four U.S. and one Canadian lock operate to bridge the 12-ft. drop from Superior to the lower lakes. The second is the seven stair-step locks at the Welland Canal which carry commerce safely around the 326-ft. Niagara escarpment.

The third, of course, is the world famous St. Lawrence Seaway . . . five Canadian and two U.S. locks which transport ships from the ports of the world into and out of the Great Lakes, carrying them 225 ft. to the Welland, at the mouth of Lake Ontario.

Sault Ste. Marie

When the new Poe Lock—the largest in the Great Lakes—opened at Sault Ste. Marie in 1969, newspapers throughout the Great Lakes region heralded the opening. The *Detroit News* called it a new standard for the future development of the St. Lawrence Seaway, noting it was the largest of any lock in the 2,342 miles between the Atlantic Ocean and the west end of Lake Superior.

The *Duluth News Tribune* called the Poe an investment in the future, remarking that the lock completed the greatest transition period in Great Lakes history, linking investments in the northern taconite-producing plants and the southern lake blast furnaces, which had been converted to handle the taconite pellets.

The New York Times pointed toward the significance of the opening of the Poe as a major event in the 10th anniversary of the opening of the Seaway.

The newest of the Sault locks was 1,200 ft. long and 110 ft. wide with a 21 ft. draft. And it made possible the construction of the land-locked super freighters, the 1,000 ft. carriers which today move taconite between the mines and processing plants in the upper lakes and the mills in the lower lakes.

The Poe was built over a period of seven years, at a cost of more than $40 million. Named after a Michigan Civil War Corps of Engineers officer, Gen. Orlando M. Poe, it became the third lock to be built in the past 114 years in the same site at the St. Marys Rapids. The first was completed in 1855 by

The Welland Canal

The four locks at Sault Ste. Marie – the Davis, Sabin, Poe and MacArthur.

Charles T. Harvey, and the second in 1896 by Gen. Poe. The present lock was under the supervision of C. A. Aune, Corpos of Engineers, at the Soo.

The second in a battery of four parallel locks, the Poe was built as a "lock within a lock." During construction, the waters of Lake Superior and Huron had to be kept out of the lock excavation in order for the builders to have a "dry hole" in which to work. At the same time, however, the other three locks in the system had to be kept operational in order to prevent Great Lakes shipping traffic from being slowed or halted. To offset this problem, coffer dams were constructed across the excavation pit at the east and west ends of the lock, and pumps were installed to keep the waters

of the upper and lower St. Marys River out of the area. The result was a pit in the center of the locking system some six city blocks long, 400 ft. wide and over 70 ft. deep.

Construction began in 1961 with the demolition of the old Poe Lock. At that point, the Corps of Engineers agreed that a planned lock of 1,000 by 100 ft. was not large enough to handle shipping of the future. So, construction was halted in 1962, while studies were conducted to reevaluate the size of the lock. The studies recommended that the Poe be extended to 1,200 ft. with a width of 110 ft., still allowing 32 ft. of water over the sills.

The McNamara Construction Co. of Canada served as prime constructor for the job on a bid of $21,471,690. Lock construction was completed in the summer of 1968 and testing of the facility occurred with the passage of the *Phillip R. Clark* on October 30.

The Sault Ste. Marie *Evening News* commented in an editorial that the new lock "means that the entire St. Lawrence Seaway System of locks will have to be one day rebuilt to allow greater flexibility of this nations' and the worlds' commerce. It means that the channels in the Great Lakes system will have to be deepened and the turns widened to handle bigger and faster boats."

The famous Sault (pronounced "Soo") had been a navigation bottleneck for the Great Lakes, of course, ever since the earliest days of water transportation. A 19 ft. falls in the St. Marys River, slight though it was, had become a barrier which ground inter-lake navigation to a complete halt. Ships downbound from Superior and upbound from the other four lakes were forced to unload their cargoes at the Sault. The cargoes were then carried overland for a full mile until they could be loaded aboard another ship, 19 ft. higher in the water.

It was in 1850 that two Michigan senators, Alpheus Felch and Lewis Cass, convinced Congress that, for the good of the region, a canal was needed at the Sault. Three years later, the Fairbanks Scale Co. and the State of Michigan signed a construction contract and within two years a lock and canal had been completed at the Sault, ending the mile-long overland portage. The canal was 5,500 ft. long—just over a mile—115 ft. high and 10 ft. thick. The canal housed two locks, each 350 ft. high and 70 ft. wide. The upper lock raised or lowered ships eight ft., the lower lock, ten ft. The cost: just $200 short of a million dollars.

Between 1876 and 1896 two new larger locks—the Weitzel and the Poe—replaced the original Michigan State locks at the Sault. The Weitzel was 515 ft. long and 80 ft. wide, while the Poe was 800 ft. long and 100 ft. wide, making it, at the time, the largest lock in the world. The two new locks this time were built by the U.S. Army Corps of Engineers, who by this time were running the Soo.

To the north of the U.S. canals, Canada later constructed a 900 ft. lock which was somewhat deeper than the Poe. Larger ships used this canal until 1914 when the 1,350 ft. Davis Lock was built. Longer than the Panama Canal locks by 350 ft., the Davis Lock was twinned before it was completed. The twin lock—the fourth for the Soo—was called the Sabin.

The four locks functioned efficiently for more than three decades, until World War II, when the smallest, the Weitzel, was replaced with a lock that matched the specifications of the Poe—800 ft. long and 80 ft. wide. It was named after General Douglas MacArthur.

In 1975 the Corps initiated a study to determine the economic value of replacing the Sabin lock with another lock the size of the Poe, or larger. The apparent need for a second large lock has arisen out of the growing construction of 1,000 ft. super carriers for use in the taconite trade from Superior to the south.

Using 1974 as a typical year to point out the cargoes that pass through the canal at Sault Ste. Marie, a commodity breakdown of cargoes would look like this:

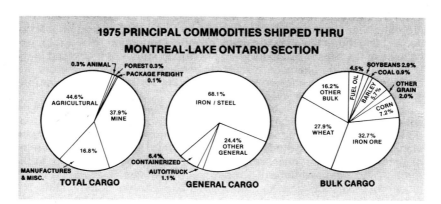

Principal commodities shipped through the Montreal-Lake Ontario section of the Seaway during 1974.

Sault Ste. Marie typical commodity movement
(year—1974)

Items	Westbound	Eastbound	Total
Wood Products			
Paper and woodpulp	—	13,059	13,059
Pulpwood, lumber and logs	—	17,674	17,674
Vegetable Products			
Wheat	9,150	11,330,535	11,339,685
Barley	—	2,391,936	2,391,936
Oats	—	564,930	564,930
Corn	3,808	1,032,316	1,036,124
Rye	—	313,487	313,487
Flaxseed	—	181,765	181,765
Soy	—	106,664	106,664
Flour	4,245	4,332	8,577
Mill products, screenings	—	615,163	615,163
Mineral Products			
Iron ore	23,660	73,869,408	73,893,068
Manufactured iron and steel	130,869	207,777	338,646
Pig iron	634	—	634
Scrap iron	—	30,474	30,474
*Stone	1,947,742	1,000	1,948,742
Cement	598,621	—	598,621
Coal	5,254,808	1,032,243	6,287,051
Nonmetallic minerals, mfrs.	183,168	—	183,168
Petroleum Products			
Gasoline	310,289	51,639	361,928
Fuel oil	686,209	43,332	729,541
Miscellaneous merchandise	613,059	282,326	895,385
Summary			
Vessel passages (Number)	7,585	5,535	13,120
Passengers (Number)	172,638	8,137	180,775
Freight (Short tons)	9,766,262	92,090,060	101,856,322

*Includes broken stone, gravel and sand.

*Source: U.S. Army Engineer District, Detroit. Corps of Engineers

An analysis of traffic for the same period of time
at the Canadian Sault Ste. Marie Canal would look like this:

Commodity Movement, 1974, Canadian Soo

Commodity (Tons)	Westbound	Eastbound	Total
Forest Products			
Paper and woodpulp	—	100,892	100,892
Pulpwood, lumber and logs	—	—	—

Agricultural Products

Wheat	—	8,947	8,947
Barley	4,700	55,598	60,298
Oats	—	34,028	34,028
Corn	—	7,949	7,949
Mill Products, Screenings	—	9,878	9,878

Mine Products

Mfg. Iron & Steel	26,599	65,574	92,173
*Stone	12,705	155,240	167,945
Coal, Bituminous	5,000	—	5,000
Coke	3,067	—	3,067
Nonmetallic minerals	37,217	—	37,217

Petroleum Products

Gasoline	31,514	30,264	61,778
Fuel Oil	56,320	35,287	91,607

Misc. Merchandise

	153,054	97,268	250,322

Summary

Vessel passages	563	2,692	3,255
Passengers	4,585	176,554	181,139
Freight 1974 season	330,176	600,925	931,101
1973 season	324,396	761,793	1,086,189

*Includes broken stone, gravel and sand

An ore carrier, hatches sealed, waits in a Sault Ste. Marie lock for water to be released so that she can continue her down-bound journey.

The Welland Canal by-pass.

The U.S. Steel vessel Philip R. Clark moves into the Soo at dusk.

The following is a comparative monthly statement of tonnage moved through Sault Ste. Marie (U.S.) during 1974:

Month	1974 Net Tons
April	5,728,380
May	12,831,934
June	13,326,153
July	13,835,959
August	10,186,195
September	9,636,893
October	11,990,903
November	10,930,430
December	8,546,029
January	2,879,059
February	865,376
March	1,099,011
	101,856,322

A unique view of vessels upbound and downbound at the Soo locks: The Louis B. Boyer and the Walter A. Sterling.

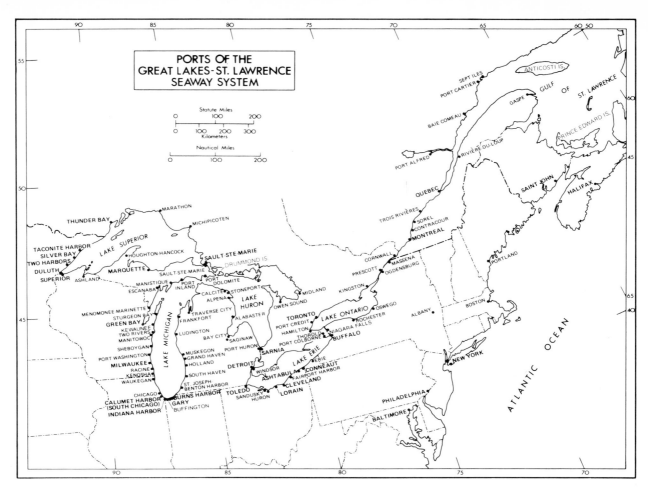

Ports of the Great Lakes-St. Lawrence Seaway system.

The St. Lawrence Seaway

A deep-draft Seaway extending along the St. Lawrence River became a serious topic of discussion as the 19th century came to a close and the experiment of the locks at Sault Ste. Marie had proved its value. The tonnage that passed through this St. Marys River minimum lock and canal operation — mostly iron ore, grain and coal — had doubled that of the Suez Canal. It seemed that the time was right to talk about building another canal — this time, one to put midwestern grain directly into the ports of Europe, breaking the strangle-hold which the railroad monopoly had for so long held over the U.S. prairie farmer.

A Swedish immigrant from Minnesota by the name of John Lind, as a legislator, called for the construction of a waterway from the Lakes to the sea. Elected to Congress by the farmers of New Ulm, Minnesota in 1892, Lind sponsored a Congressional resolution to provide for a joint U.S.-Canadian investigation into the possibility of improving water transportation from the head of Lake Superior to the sea. His initial legislation led—after decades of bitter opposition—to the construction of the St. Lawrence Seaway more than half a century later.

A Seaway would court economic disaster such as the nation had never seen, arch-foes to the proposed system told the American people and the Congress.

"The operation of the Seaway will result in the loss of a coal market for American coal mines, amounting to 17 million tons annually—avery serious matter for American labor," Dr. Louis Haney, an economist for the Mississippi Valley Association reported. "It will admit cheap foreign coal into the Great Lakes region." He predicted ominous impacts that a route to the sea would have for America. Because foreign tramp steamers would use the Seaway, they would make mid-continent America a dumping ground for cheap products from foreign countries.

It wasn't until the second half of the century, when great new iron ore fields were discovered in the Labrador wilderness—an iron strike comparable to the discovery of the great Mesabi range in the United States—that a St.

Lawrence Seaway gained the support it needed to win acceptance from big industry.

The steel companies, and the lake fleets which they owned, now saw rising out of the transport of the Labrador ore a strong profit and a value in the construction of a Seaway. The St. Lawrence waterway suddenly became, for the steel interests, a logical way to carry ore from wilderness to mills. So, big steel became a contributor to the support for a Seaway and, with it, the here-to-for anti-Seaway Lake Carrier's Association came out strongly in favor of the waterway.

Major General Bernard L. Robinson, Chief Deputy of Engineers for the U.S. Army told the House Public Works Committee, headed by Minnesota's legendary John Blatnik, that, "The St. Lawrence Seaway, with a 27 ft. chan-

Ocean vessel upbound from the Atlantic Ocean at night in the St. Lawrence Seaway.

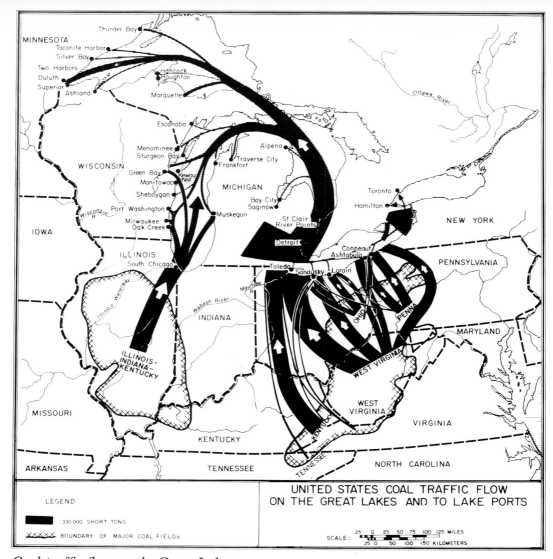

Coal traffic flow on the Great Lakes.

nel depth, will contribute greatly to our national security, as well as to our peacetime economy. It is economically justified . . . It will be a self-liquidating project, paying its own way without placing a burden on our taxpayers. *Moreover, it is a project that will be built by Canada alone, if we fail to take advantage of this . . . opportunity to participate in its construction. Such unilateral action would not be in the best interests of this nation, from either defense or commercial consideration."*

In April 1953, President Dwight Eisenhower wrote to Senator Alexander Wiley, "At my request, the National Security Council has considered the national interests in the Great Lakes-St. Lawrence Seaway project. The Council has advised me (that) the early initiation and completion of the St.

Lawrence-Great Lakes Seaway is in the interests of national security, (and that) the United States should promptly take whatever action may be appropriate to clear the way for commencement of the project, whether by Canada alone or as may be better developed by Canada and the United States jointly."

There were always arguments against the Seaway. The powerful Chicago Association of Commerce and Industry stated that the Great Lakes-St. Lawrence Seaway and Power Project was not necessary at all, and in the interests of national defense, might acutally be injurious to the American defense efforts. It postulated that (1) Lake Superior district resources of iron ore are "sufficient to supply Great Lakes steel producing plants far into the future," (2) eastern steel producing areas

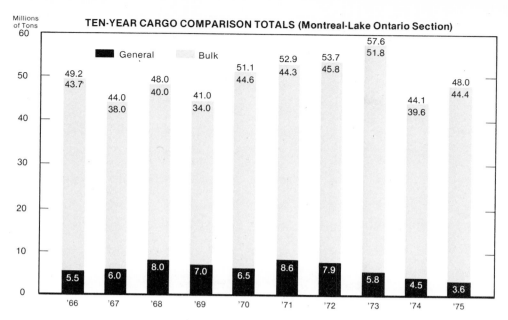

TEN-YEAR CARGO COMPARISON TOTALS (Montreal-Lake Ontario Section)

Millions of Tons

■ General   ▓ Bulk

Year	Bulk	General
'66	43.7 (49.2)	5.5
'67	38.0 (44.0)	6.0
'68	40.0 (48.0)	8.0
'69	34.0 (41.0)	7.0
'70	44.6 (51.1)	6.5
'71	44.3 (52.9)	8.6
'72	45.8 (53.7)	7.9
'73	51.8 (57.6)	5.8
'74	39.6 (44.1)	4.5
'75	44.4 (48.0)	3.6

A ten year comparison totals of bulk and general cargo for the Montreal-Lake Ontario section of the St. Lawrence Seaway.

Anticipated iron ore traffic by 1995. (Source U.S. Bureau of Mines)

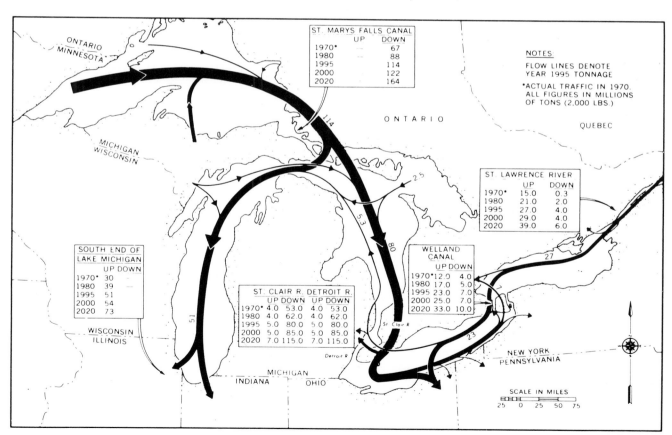

could "more effectively use imported ore" and (3) the Seaway would "not be needed for those purposes at all."

The Chicago group also noted that there was no need for the movement of ships into or out of the Great Lakes for construction or repair, no need to expand shipbuilding facilities when there were ample facilities at tidewater shipyards.

Thomas A. Murray, New York State Chairman of the American Federation of Labor said, "The harmful effect of the proposed Seaway on labor is beyond calculation."

But despite continuous opposition — opposition which lasted for over 50 years — from powerful east and gulf coast ports, railroads, power brokers and financial centers along the eastern coast—finally, thanks to the efforts of a few dedicated legislators, a Seaway bill was passed.

After defeats in legislatures of 1918, 1934, 1942, 1944, 1948 and 1952, after Canadian delays in 1914, 1922 and procrastination in the entire decade of 1920-1930, a joint U.S.-Canadian Seaway became a reality in 1954 with the passage by Congress of the Wiley-Dondero Seaway Act.

The physical task of building the Seaway was immense. Each section of the 112-mile construction site developed its own seemingly unsurmountable obstacles. After five years and the dredging of over 360 million tons of

The Frank A. Sherman *awaits at the wall heading upbound toward the Great Lakes as a vessel approaches a Seaway lock in high water.*

It is easy to see why they are called long boats.

rock, after the resettlement of thousands of people and entire towns, after changing the face of the earth and the homes and habits of thousands of its inhabitants—seven new locks and the world's largest joint power facility were completed.

Today, the agricultural and industrial greatness of the Seaway region—from the water gateway at Montreal to the lakehead ports of Superior and Michigan—is unequalled in any other areas of the world. The five lakes with 95,000 square miles of navigable waters, serve some 50 ports that handle millions of tons of cargo annually, from a tributary hinterland area of 17 states and four provinces.

From Montreal to Lake Ontario a vessel rises more than 225 feet. This 182-mile stretch of waterway is comprised of five legal sections, three of which are solely in Canadian waters.

The first of these sections, some 31 miles long, enables marine traffic to bypass the Lachine Rapids. Two locks—the St. Lambert,

opposite Montreal and the Cote Ste. Catherine, eight and a half miles upstream—are employed to raise vessels 50 ft. to the level of Lake St. Louis, a wide section of the St. Lawrence at the confluence with the Ottawa River.

Beyond Lake St. Louis, vessels enter the second section, the Soulanges, a 16-mile stretch which includes the two Beauharnois locks, providing a total lift of about 85 feet.

The third section, 29 miles in length, terminates east of Cornwall, Ontario. It is the last of the three all-Canadian sections in the Montreal-Lake Ontario part of the Seaway.

The international segment is entered at the head of Lake St. Francis and extends to a point east of Ogdensburg, New York. Previously a swift-flowing section of the river, it was converted into a broad lake by the Moses-Saunders Power Dam. Differences in elevation here are overcome by the United States' Eisenhower and Snell locks near Massena, New York and by the Canadian control lock at Iroquois, Ontario.

*The Iroquois lock, the most westerly of the seven
Seaway locks between Montreal and Ontario.*

Lower Beauharnois lock.

Cote Ste. Catherine lock.

Upper Beauharnois lock.

St. Lambert lock.

U.S. Snell (top) and Eisenhower (below) locks.

Studies of wave action conducted by the Seaway Corporation as a protection to the shoreline frequently results in reduced speeds through certain channels at times of high water.

At the lower end of this section, the Seaway route bypasses the Moses-Saunders Power Dam, which was built in conjunction with the Seaway project and lies astride the U.S.-Canadian international boundary. Owned equally by Ontario Hydro (Canada) and the Power Authority of the State of New York, the facility has a generating capacity of some 1.8 million kilowatts.

The remaining 68 miles of the St. Lawrence, the Thousand Islands section, is open channel and free of rapids, although many rock shoals were removed to provide the 27 foot navigation channel.

Access to the eastern end of Lake Erie, barred by Niagara Falls, is provided through the 27-mile Welland Canal, which has seven locks (and one guard lock) to lift vessels some 326 feet into Lake Erie.

How do the Seaway locks work? How does a ship actually climb to the height of a 60-story skyscraper on the water route from the tidewater to the clear, fresh water of Lake Superior? Like this:

All of the locks on the St. Lawrence Seaway are filled or emptied by gravity. To raise a vessel, the upstream valves of the lock are opened and the water simply flows into the chamber through openings at the bottom of the walls.

1. From the lower level, the ship sails through the open gates into the lock. The vessel secures itself to bollards on the side of the walls. The gates are closed.

2. The valves are opened and water is allowed to flow in, lifting the ship.

3. When the vessel reaches the higher level, the upper gates are opened and the ship sails out.

To lower a vessel the steps are reversed. It takes less than 10 minutes to raise or lower the water level of a lock, with more than 20 million gallons used for each lockage. Additional time is required for the vessel to maneuver in and out of the lock chamber. The average lockage requires approximately 33 minutes from the time the bow of the ship passes the approach wall until the stern is cleared of the outermost boom.

The St. Lawrence Seaway Development Corporation (SLSDC), as a wholly-owned government corporation, was established to develop, operate and maintain that portion of the St. Lawrence Seaway in the United States' territorial waters. Originally a part of the Department of Commerce, SLSDC was later transferred to its more logical position as a modal administration within the Department of Transportation.

The St. Lawrence Seaway Authority is the Canadian counterpart agency, operating the other five Seaway locks as well as the Canadian lock at Sault Ste. Marie.

All seven Seaway locks are 766 ft. in length from breast well to gate fender, meaning that ships entering the locks must be no longer than 730 ft. Each lock is 80 ft. wide, with a depth over sills of 300 ft. deep.

Proceeding eastward, or downbound, from the Lakes to the sea, the first of the St. Lawrence locks is the Iroquois, which lowers ships from 5 to 6 ft. downstream. Nearby Eisenhower Lock lowers ships from 38 to 42 ft. and its companion, the Snell Lock, 45 to 49 ft. The Beauharnois, next in the chain, lowers ships 36 to 40 and 38 to 42 feet respectively for the upper and lower lock. Cote Ste. Catherine drops the ships another 33 to 35 feet, and the last lock out to the sea, St. Lambert, drops them a final 13 to 20 ft. to tidewater.

The Canadian Seaway Authority is responsible for the billing and collecting of all tolls. Revenue division between the United States and Canada is 73% to Canada and 27% to the United States for a full transit of the Seaway. The Seaway entities pay all of their operating expenses from toll revenues, returning net operating income — their profits — to their governments to pay for the cost of construction.

Data on the Great Lakes

Lake Superior

Area (Sq. Mi.)	31,800
Shoreline (Miles)	1,500
Length (Miles)	350
Depth (Ft.)	1,290
Width (Miles)	160
Above Sea Level (Ft.)	601.6
Above Lake Ontario (Ft.)	357.6

Lake Michigan

Area (Sq. Mi.)	22,400
Shoreline (Miles)	1,200
Length (Miles)	310
Depth (Ft.)	923
Width (Miles)	118
Above Sea Level (Ft.)	578.5
Above Lake Ontario (Ft.)	334.5

Lake Huron

Area (Sq. Mi.)	23,200
Shoreline (Miles)	800
Length (Miles)	220
Depth (Ft.)	750
Width (Miles)	100
Above Sea Level (Ft.)	578.5
Above Lake Ontario (Ft.)	334.5

Lake Erie

Area (Sq. Mi.)	9,932
Shoreline (Miles)	650
Length (Miles)	240
Depth (Ft.)	210
Width (Miles)	57
Above Sea Level (Ft.)	570.5
Above Lake Ontario (Ft.)	326.0

Lake Ontario

Area (Sq. Mi.)	7,540
Shoreline (Miles)	500
Length (Miles)	190
Depth (Ft.)	778
Width (Miles)	55
Above Sea Level (Ft.)	244.0

A Great Lakes floating dry dock at Detroit is operated by Nicholson Terminal. Here a vessel is removed from the water as repairmen inspect her propeller shaft.

Welland and St. Lawrence Canals:
Traffic Volumes and Number of Transits

Year	Welland Canal			St. Lawrence Seaway		
	Net tons of Freight (000)	Number of Transits	Average tons per Transit	Net tons of Freight (000)	Number of Transits	Average tons per Transit
1950 (pre-	14,741	7,436	1,982	9,669	10,147	953
1958 Seaway)	21,274	8,736	2,435	11,762	11,184	1,052
1959	27,156	8,252	3,291	20,352	7,590	2,681
1960	29,250	7,536	3,881	20,310	6,869	2,957
1961	31,455	7,747	4,060	23,418	6,892	3,398
1962	35,406	7,615	4,650	25,594	6,351	4,030
1963	41,303	7,597	5,473	30,943	6,285	4,923
1964	51,389	8,304	6,188	39,309	6,779	5,799
1965	53,420	8,384	6,372	43,383	7,330	5,919
1966	59,272	8,714	6,802	49,249	7,341	6,709
1967	52,809	7,437	7,101	44,029	6,921	6,362
1968	58,075	7,204	8,061	47,954	6,576	7,292
1969	53,532	6,863	7,800	41,014	6,392	6,416
1970	62,963	7,111	8,854	51,143	6,277	8,148
1971	62,909	6,854	9,178	52,948	6,059	8,739
1972	64,095	6,768	9,470	53,580	5,936	9,026
1973	67,195	6,815	9,860	57,634	6,125	9,410
1974	52,360	5,171	10,126	44,146	4,260	10,363

Source: St. Lawrence Seaway Authority. Annual Report

St. Lawrence River Section

Locks:
— Proceeding upbound a vessel must clear seven locks between Montreal and Lake Ontario: St. Lambert, Cote Ste. Catherin, Lower Beauharnois, Upper Beauharnois, Snell, Eisenhower and Iroquois. The Snell and Eisenhower locks are maintained, owned and operated by the SLSDC; other locks are Canadian.

Lock Specifications:
— Length, gate to gate - 860'
— Width - 80'
— Depth over sills - 30'

Controlling Height:
Masts must not exceed 117' above water level

Average Lockage Time/Commercial Ship:
30 minutes

Average Cargo/Loaded Commercial Transit (1975):
13,756 tons

1975 Container Traffic:
14,988 containers

Average Transit Time (Montreal-Lake Ontario, Tibbets Pt.):
21 hours

System-Wide Data (Great Lakes and St. Lawrence River):

Selected Distances:
— 8,300 miles of shoreline
— 2,342 miles, Atlantic to Duluth
— 2,250 miles, Atlantic to Chicago
— 1,000 miles, Atlantic to Montreal
— 182 miles, Montreal to Lake Ontario

Typical System-Long Voyage (Montreal to Duluth):
1,342 miles over which vessel would clear 16 locks that would raise or lower it approximately 600 ft. Besides 7 locks in St. Law-

rence River, ship would clear 8 Canadian locks ($100/lock) at Welland Canal—between Lakes Ontario and Erie; and one of four U.S. Army Corps of Engineers locks or Canadian lock (no charge) at Sault Ste. Marie—between Lakes Huron and Superior.

Shipping Season Duration:
April through December, St. Lawrence River and Welland Canal; year-round in upper Great Lakes.

Major Bulk Commodities Shipped:
Iron ore, coal and grain.

Major General Cargo Shipped:
Iron and steel products and manufactured goods.

Associate Administrator and Resident Manager of the Seaway, William Kennedy presents a photograph depicting a Seaway scene to Congressman Robert C. McEwen, the Congressional representative from the area which geographically houses the Seaway.

Opening and Closing Dates at Critical Points of the Great Lakes-St. Lawrence Seaway System, 1958-1976

	St. Lawrence Canal		Welland Ship Canal		Sault Ste. Marie Locks		Straits of Mackinac	
	First Passage	Last Passage	First Passage	Last Passage	First Passage	Last Passage	First Passage	Last Passage
1958	April 14[1]	Dec. 19[1]	April 1	Dec. 18	April 17	Dec. 14	March 28	Dec. 17
1959	April 25	Dec. 3	April 6	Dec. 15	April 14	Dec. 21	April 4	Dec. 25
1960	April 18	Dec. 3	April 1	Dec. 15	April 7	Dec. 15	April 4	Dec. 18
1961	April 11	Nov. 30	April 1	Dec. 15	April 8	Dec. 17	March 20	Jan. 10, 1962
1962	April 23	Dec. 7	April 1	Dec. 15	April 7	Dec. 19	April 9	Dec. 29
1963	April 15	Dec. 13	April 7	Dec. 18	April 15	Dec. 20	April 15	Dec. 27
1964	April 8	Dec. 7	March 30	Dec. 15	April 1	Dec. 16	March 18	Dec. 22
1965	April 8	Dec. 17	April 1	Dec. 16	April 14	Dec. 18	March 25	Jan. 16, 1966
1966	April 1	Dec. 15	April 4	Dec. 15	April 1	Dec. 20	March 20	Jan. 12, 1967
1967	April 7	Dec. 15	April 1	Dec. 16	April 10	Dec. 30	March 30	Jan. 16, 1968
1968	April 18	Dec. 15	April 1	Dec. 22	April 2	Jan. 4, 1969	March 30	Jan. 4, 1969
1969	April 7	Dec. 15	April 1	Dec. 22	April 4	Jan. 11, 1970	March 21	Jan. 10, 1970
1970	April 4	Dec. 17	April 1	Dec. 30	April 1	Jan. 29, 1971	March 30	Jan. 30, 1971
1971	April 14	Dec. 18	April 1	Dec. 16	April 8	Feb. 1, 1972	March 26	Feb. 1, 1972
1972	April 12	Dec. 23	April 3	Dec. 16	April 10	Feb. 8, 1973	March 28	Feb. 8, 1973
1973	Mar. 28	Dec. 22	March 27	Jan. 4, 1974	March 28	Feb. 7, 1974	March 19	Feb. 21, 1974
1974	Mar. 26	Dec. 17	March 21	Jan. 17, 1975	April 12	*	March 26	*
1975	Mar. 25	Dec. 19	March 25	Dec. 31	*	*	*	*
1976	April 4	Dec. 24	April 1	Jan. 3, 1977	*	Jan 21, 1977	*	*

[1]Pre-Seaway Coral System
*No Closing — Open All Year

Sources:

For St. Lawrence Canals and Welland Ship Canal 1958-1970: *U.S. Army Corps of Engineers Survey Report on Great Lakes and St. Lawrence Seaway Navigation Season Extension,* Detroit District, Dec. 1969. Other: Lake Carrier's Association, *Annual Report,* 1958 through 1974, Great Lakes Commission.

A self-unloader uses its conveyor to transfer cargo to shore. Note figure on top of conveyor.

7

Cargoes of the Carriers

As transportation on the Great Lakes developed in the last half of the nineteenth century, industrial progress in the midcontinent followed at a rapid rate. Throughout the Great Lakes region, industry thrived. Workers from all parts of the world came to the steel and flour mills, coal mines, stone quarries, factories and the stockyards of the Great Lakes region. By the turn of the century, America's industrial heartland was its midwest: Chicago, Gary, Detroit, Toledo, Lorain, Cleveland, Pittsburgh, Youngstown, Erie, Buffalo—metropolitan areas which soon became the giant production and distribution centers of the greatest manufacturing region the world has ever known.

The vast iron ranges of the Lake Superior region—the Mesabi, Menominee, Cuyuna and others—set the stage for the might, and ultimately the industrial greatness of the Great Lakes region. The birth of the mills, and ultimately the giant steel complexes of the southern Lakes region gave rise to, and in turn were created by, the low cost and efficient water transportation of the Lakes.

When high grade iron ore deposits began diminishing, investment initially in research and later for processing operations—close to two billion dollars worth—were made by the iron mining industry in the Superior area. The result was a sharp upgrading of both standard and low grade ores to meet the specifications of the blast furnaces. Today, more than 75% of the ore shipped from the ranges of

the north are in the form of pellets made by a concentration process using taconite or jasper. From low grade iron bearing rocks deposited there millions of years ago in almost unlimited quantities, pellets are today created which contain more than 62% iron and are considered actually to be superior blast furnace material.

At a taconite processing plant in Minnesota, crushers grind chunks of rock-hard taconite into pieces approximately one inch in diameter. Rod-and-ball mills then reduce the iron ore into smaller particles and magnets separate out the magnetic iron. The ore, now about the consistency of flour, is fed into drums where it is rolled into pellets about the size of small marbles and baked to make them hard and uniform.

In upgrading non-magnetic jasper ore in Michigan, iron is freed by a floatation process: About three tons of crude ore are needed to produce a ton of pellets. Experiments now underway with other low grade ores (such as semi-taconite) will determine whether they also can economically be processed into pellets. Ultimately, concentrates made from these ores are expected to add still further to the output of high grade ore pellets, whose transportation requires a strong and growing Great Lakes fleet.

The iron-rich north country which the Great Lakes fleet serves was discovered in 1845 when a government surveyor named William A. Burt found surface ore in the Lake

Loading equipment silhouettes against the after-noon sky.

Dry bulk cargo loading.

Loading ore.

Superior region. In the late 1880's a family named Merritt located the fabulous Mesabi range, where high grade ore—up to 64%—was assayed.

(The Mesabi lies in what is known as the Minnesota Arrow Head, a section of the United States which juts prominently beyond normal border lines and into Canada. How did the U.S. obtain this land—and ultimately the Mesabi range? In England, in 1775, a map of the British Colonies was drawn by Dr. John Mitchell, a map that was later used to establish the international boundary. At the head of the Great Lakes, he followed the Pigeon River as a boundary while, historians say, he might just as easily—and more logically—have used the St. Louis River out of the Duluth. Another story tells that Benjamin Franklin established the boundary line of the

new country, choosing this same northern-most river that flowed into the Great Lakes and then spread, fan shape, into the wilderness. The section of the fan that became part of the United States contained the Mesabi and other great iron ranges.)

The Mesabi range was not immediately developed by the Merritts because they could not find the major financial backing necessary to develop their newly discovered mines, and they began operating the mine with limited, local financing. Eastern interests discovered the value of the mines and later moved in. After years of involvement and entanglement, the Merritts lost all of their holdings and died poor. The Mesabi was then developed and millionaires were made many times over.

In another area, a German by the name of Frank Hibbing dug a water well and found

The Frank Purnell.

Canada Steamships' latest self-unloader, J.W. McGiffin.

Ore carrier unloads taconite.

Numbered chutes open, dropping coal into hull.

The Amoco Oil Company's 400-ft. Amoco Wisconsin, *a familiar Great Lakes tanker.*

The 392-foot S.T. Crapo, *the only vessel specifically designed for the cement trade.*

virtually a mountain of ore. The ore—at what is today Hibbing, Minnesota—was to become recognized as the richest to be found anywhere in the world.

Most of the mines in the iron ranges today were worked by the open pit method, in which the earth was stripped off by power shovels. Long conveyor belts move the ore to surface plants for conversion into pellets and loading into railway cars for a journey to the loading docks.

Loading and unloading cargo a century ago bore very little resemblance to the methods used today. Ore was loaded by hand into barrels and stowed in the holds of the vessels. Later, it was carried by wheelbarrows along platforms above the holds and dumped. The unloaded ore was shoveled into buckets which were raised by ropes.

Today bulk cargoes normally require little or no manual labor in direct handling. Newer lakers even carry small deck cranes which handle their steel hatch covers. The cranes move on rails which run the length of the deck.

Now, loading and unloading has become a science, with special equipment developed for the handling of each commodity. Ports have become renouned for handling a particular commodity in volume. For instance, Superior is known for iron ore, Duluth, Minnesota for grain, Toledo and Conneaut, Ohio for coal and Calcite, Michigan for limestone.

Loading and unloading efficiencies, of course, have direct bearings on transportation costs. Obviously, the less time a vessel spends in port, the more time it has to make more trips.

Shipping docks are usually immense—provide berthing for vessels, cargo handling and storage areas, along with railroad car loading and unloading systems, storage and stockpiling facilities. Some ore loading docks are nearly 80 ft. high, half a mile long and can berth six vessels at a time. Railroad cars run on top of such docks to fill "pockets" later emptied through shoots directly into the vessels holds.

Newer docks, built specifically for unloading taconite pellets, are not as spectacular in their dimensions, but they are equally impressive with their performance, loading thousands of tons in a few hours with precise conveyor belt systems. Coal loading docks tower high above vessel decks where great conveyors and chutes move thousands of tons of coal an hour, quickly and efficiently. The equivalent of millions of barrels of bulk cement is also carried by Great Lakes vessels, as are millions of bushels of grain which flow from mammoth silos and grain elevators by the water.

The unloading equipment best known in the Lakes are the Huletts. Named for Cleveland's George Hulett, the unloader consists of a control cab mounted on top of bucket jaws. This configuration rests at the end of a long arm connected to a massive base that rides on tracks at the dock. An operator actually rides the jaw into the ship's hold, taking a 15 to 18 ton bite of cargo and moving upwards again, to where the cargo is dumped.

Most of the unloading ore ports on the Lakes use the fast, efficient Hulett unloaders.

Ore such as taconite can also be handled easily by equipment aboard ship. Previously,

Grain is loaded aboard the Quebecois.

The 650-ft. Algoway, *owned by Algoma Central Railway, built in 1972.*

Aerial view of grain elevators at Thunder Bay.

Cargo is unloaded from ore carrier directly into hold of ocean vessel.

Loading system at grain elevators.

The mills of lower Lake Michigan.

self-unloaders were used only in specialized service and were not as popular as they are today. The concept was pioneered in 1908 by the Wyandotte Transportation Company which was met with ridicule with the idea of such a ridiculous looking self-unloading vessel. The first self-unloader was a success, however, and three more "ridiculous" vessels were added to the Wyandotte Line by 1916.

In 1923, the Canadians took a long look at the self-unloader concept and its Glen Line took delivery of the first canal size self-unloader. Five or six years later, Canada Steamship Lines converted a vessel to become a self-unloader and from then on, the concept took hold—and now, all new Canadian bulk carriers are so constructed.

The Canadians have built different types of self-unloaders: some feature drag scrapers which collect cargo for discharge into elevators, with the bulk cargo moving them along conveyor booms and over the side of the vessel. Most unloaders are built with a conveyor belt running the length of the ship.

As many as three belts are used with booms supported by an *A frame*. At this writing, in Canada, the Algoma Central fleet includes seven self-unloaders; Bayswater, five; Canada Steamship Lines, 14; Ore Carriers, two; Great Lakes Transportation Co., one; Hall Corp., seven; International Waterways, Eugene

Lafebre, Scott Misener, Tee Transit, Valley Kamp Coal Co., one each; R.E. Law Crushed Stone, two; Upper Great Lakes Shipping, four; Westdale Shipping, eight.

Many of the large shipping companies' customers, such as utility and steel operations are not installing costly unloading equipment in their new facilities. This fact gives the business of the newer power generating and steel complexes to fleets which operate self-unloaders.

All new super carriers, as a matter of fact (ships about 1,000 ft. long, with a capacity of 50,000 tons), are self-unloaders. It appears obvious that as the self-unloaders' share of the total transportation market increases, bulkers will probably be converted, retired or confined to the minor trades.

It costs about a third more to build a self-unloader than a straight bulker, but the former earns a rate premium of about 5% and is able to make faster turn-arounds and, thereby, more trips in a season.

Special handling equipment which has been developed for the Great Lakes vessels often make it possible to tell the cargo a vessel is carrying simply by her silhouette — by the types of booms or cranes, or by their absence.

Bulk cargo tonnages handled by the Great Lakes fleet in the past three decades can be seen in the chart below:

The William A. Reiss, *owned by Oglebay Norton.*

Carrier prepares for loading.

THIRTY YEAR TABLE OF LAKE BULK FREIGHT COMMERCE

	Iron Ore Gross Tons	Soft and Hard Coal Net Tons	Grain of Various Kinds Net Tons	Stone Net Tons	Total Net Tons
1945	75,714,750	55,246,197	18,717,773	16,318,193	175,082,683
1946	59,356,716	53,726,531	10,197,850	17,551,555	147,955,458
1947	77,898,087	58,059,884	11,409,228	20,891,130	177,606,099
1948	82,937,192	60,563,530	9,876,880	22,282,425	185,612,490
1949	69,556,269	40,929,565	12,542,565	20,322,136	151,697,287
1950	78,205,592	57,640,222	9,327,450	23,395,011	177,952,976
1951	89,092,012	50,945,656	13,150,144	25,871,319	189,750,172
1952	74,910,798	46,284,192	15,214,778	23,277,942	168,677,006
1953	95,844,449	51,034,713	14,317,229	26,999,207	199,696,932
1954	60,793,697	46,367,167	11,866,241	24,975,440	151,297,789
1955	89,169,973	53,378,385	10,787,786	29,722,293	193,758,833
1956	80,195,929	57,374,685	14,319,650	30,753,412	192,267,187
1957	87,278,815	56,779,772	11,234,810	30,439,375	196,206,230
1958	54,787,479	44,949,995	12,625,829	22,496,239	141,434,040
1959	51,450,731	47,228,449	13,609,452	26,159,660	144,622,380
1960	73,073,053	46,701,235	14,134,959	27,179,458	169,857,471
1961	60,897,367	43,969,665	16,607,745	25,418,364	154,200,725
1962	63,085,330	46,184,285	15,918,950	24,730,834	157,489,639
1963	67,298,000	51,642,796	18,777,164	28,547,128	174,440,849
1964	78,115,327	52,142,742	21,637,255	30,771,477	192,040,640
1965	78,627,591	54,574,092	21,875,439	30,819,351	195,331,784
1966	85,273,676	55,585,464	25,013,943	34,021,957	210,127,881
1967	80,605,929	52,890,668	17,616,863	31,716,614	192,502,786
1968	83,631,049	48,861,866	16,325,298	33,093,501	191,947,440
1969	86,307,605	46,924,447	16,594,713	36,083,477	196,267,146
1970	87,018,233	49,683,710	23,820,347	38,477,439	209,531,517
1971	78,162,234	43,341,847	25,239,080	33,998,558	190,131,586
1972	81,158,094	43,235,484	26,692,466	37,345,901	198,170,916
1973	94,545,275	39,604,341	26,536,921	42,888,052	214,920,023
1974	87,577,977	34,989,243	19,589,153	43,096,337	195,762,067

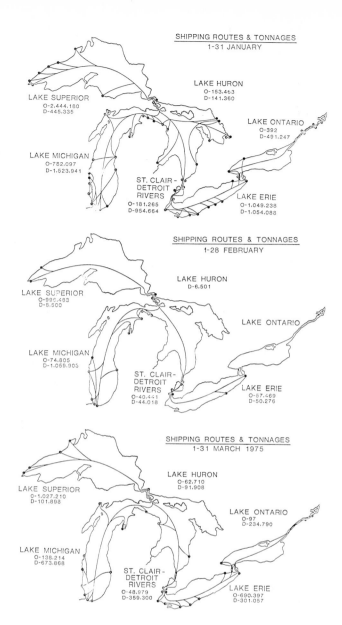

SHIPPING ROUTES & TONNAGES
1-31 JANUARY

LAKE HURON
O-153,463
D-141,360

LAKE ONTARIO
O-392
D-491,247

LAKE SUPERIOR
O-2,444,180
D-445,335

LAKE MICHIGAN
O-782,097
D-1,523,941

ST. CLAIR-
DETROIT
RIVERS
O-181,265
D-954,664

LAKE ERIE
O-1,049,238
D-1,054,088

SHIPPING ROUTES & TONNAGES
1-28 FEBRUARY

LAKE HURON
D-6,501

LAKE ONTARIO

LAKE SUPERIOR
O-996,483
D-8,500

LAKE MICHIGAN
O-74,805
D-1,059,905

ST. CLAIR-
DETROIT
RIVERS
O-40,441
D-44,018

LAKE ERIE
O-57,469
D-50,276

SHIPPING ROUTES & TONNAGES
1-31 MARCH 1975

LAKE HURON
O-62,710
D-91,908

LAKE ONTARIO
O-97
D-234,790

LAKE SUPERIOR
O-1,027,210
D-101,898

LAKE MICHIGAN
O-138,214
D-673,868

ST. CLAIR-
DETROIT
RIVERS
O-48,979
D-359,300

LAKE ERIE
O-690,397
D-301,057

The late-winter shipping routes during the winter navigation Demonstration Program are seen in these three maps which show routes during the months of January (top) February (middle) and March (bottom).

Operation Taconite, operating between Two Harbors and the lower mills of Lake Michigan.

Current expectations indicate that the need for taconite will increase at the rate of at least 20,000,000 tons per year, over current requirements, by 1980. New pelletizing plants are now under construction in the upper Michigan and Minnesota iron ore ranges in anticipation of this demand.

Dry bulk cargoes account for most of the traffic carried in Canadian Great Lakes vessels. In 1973 this accounted for over 77 million tons of freight, generating some 58.8 billion ton miles within a nine month shipping season. Grain, iron ore and coal accounted for 73.9 million tons of 83% of this total. Salt and stone account for the major portion of the remainder, with gypsum, cement, newsprint, coke and pig iron comprising the rest of the total.

The predominant grain movement for Canada runs from Thunder Bay to the St. Lawrence River ports of Montreal, Trois Riviers, Sorel, Quebec, Baie-Comeau and Port Cartier. Grain movement between Thunder Bay and Georgian Bay ports is still important for Canada.

A typical Canadian laker will travel downbound through the Lakes carrying coal or grain and up-bound it will carry ore. The availability of one of these cargoes effects the rate at which the other will be transported, because of the loss of one means costly movement in ballast.

Bustling Detroit Marine Terminal at Detroit.

Taconite and snow – a good mix.

Clam shell dips into laker hull.

Railroad car can be seen on vessel to right of crane at this unloading dock.

A cement dock.

The Bethlehem Steel plant is in the background at the Port of Indiana facility.

Small locomotive is surrounded by empty cars at yards, awaiting loading.

Bulldozer has been lowered into hull of carrier to gather remaining cargo for clam shell unloader.

Bridge of an ore carrier.

Radio and electronic controls.

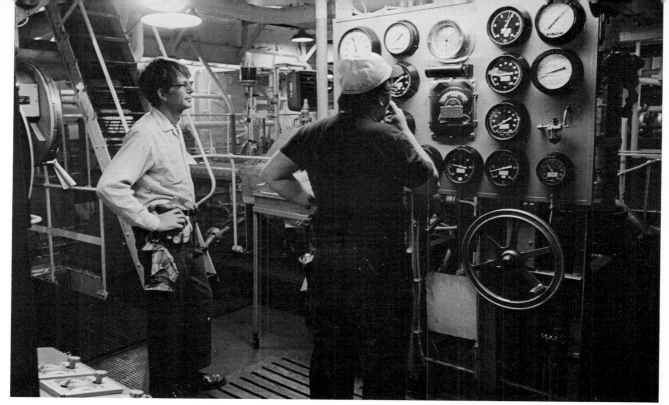

Engine crew at work.

Crews

A laker carries between 28 and 40 men. At the forward end of the vessel are the living quarters for the captain, mate, wheelsman and deck crew, while cabins at aft quarter the chief engineer, his assistants and engine room personnel. Also aft are the galleys and dining rooms and quarters for the chief steward and his helpers.

Quarters are comfortably furnished. When crews are off watch, the men have well equipped recreation rooms at their disposal. The Lake Carriers' Association points to the "healthy, clean and vigorous life" of the Great Lakes sailor. His normal working year lasts about nine months, LCA states, from the time he helps fit out his vessel in the spring until

The days of the sailor are more complex now.

The crewman's life is a hardy one. The work is difficult, but the food is among the best served any-where, and the galley on an ore carrier is equipped with equipment as fine as that in most restaurants.

late in the fall. He is well paid and has many attractive employee benefits, comparable to those of any shore industry and because meals and quarters are furnished at no cost, many are able to save most of their season's pay.

"The career Great Lakes sailor is most likely a family man with family responsibilities," the Lake Carriers' Association reports. "From the first time he steps onto a ship he begins to fit into one of the smoothest working transportation systems in the world."

Chances are that he loves his life aboard ship and has a genuine pride in the traditions of the life at sea in the Great Lakes. According to Vice Admiral Paul Trimble, Ret. President of the Lake Carriers' Association, "A good worker, alert and ambitious, can become an officer, chief engineer or even a captain. A seaman seeking promotion may supplement his practical experience by attending winter classes in navigation or marine engineering sponsored by the Association."

Rigging the lights during a Great Lakes blizzard.

This boom will carry the seaman to the wall of the lock below, where he will secure the vessel until it becomes her turn to transit the Seaway Locks.

Confidence, skill and devotion to duty is written in the faces of these Great Lakes sailors.

Ships officer heads for the bridge. Dress for the Great Lakes is usually this informal.

Good food on the Great Lakes in a tradition that has grown with the maritime industry. It is a well known fact that many chief stewards are widely known throughout the Great Lakes for their excellent meals and enjoy the prestige and status near that of a chief in a fine hotel.

"For the Great Lakes sailor," Trimble says, "there is a constant thrill in the everchanging panorama of the Great Lakes. To pass swiftly by the summer colonies in the St. Clair flats, to sail under the Blue Water Bridge into Lake Huron or through the Mackinac Bridge from Lake Michigan . . . to lock through the Sault sailing around Whitefish past the Keweenaw Peninsula, and finally approach, by night, Duluth's jeweled horseshoe of lights are experiences never to be forgotten."

A Just-Completed Great Lakes Test
Validates a New Commercial Energy Source

The nation's first full-scale test of the commercial use of oil processed from shale rock took place on the Great Lakes, and has been called an overwhelming success.

Using oil refined from the Navy Oil Shale Reserves near Rifle, Col., the Cleveland Cliffs oil carrier *Edward B. Greene* conducted a seven-day test of the fuel.

The heavy fuel used by the *Greene* was one of seven different fuel types produced from the Paraho Oil Shale Development Project on the Navy's oil reserves. Both the Navy and private industry are anxious to develop shale oil recovery processes that are commercially feasible.

Oil shale comes from a marlstone containing an organic material called kerogen. When heated to about 900 degrees Farenheit in a retort, kerogen yields shale oil, a synthetic crude that is low in sulphur and capable of being refined into most petroleum products.

The companies involved in the project include: Standard Oil Co. (Ohio), Southern California Edison Co., Mobil Oil Corp. and Cleveland-Cliffs Iron Co.

The test was coordinated by the U.S. Navy in cooperation with the Coast Guard's Office of Research and Development, Cleveland-Cliffs and the Maritime Association Division of Great Lakes Shipping.

Cleveland-Cliffs' Marine Division chief, John L. Horton said the company was impressed by the initial test results, adding that they demonstrated some definite economies to using shale oil for maritime and other industry applications.

"In fact," he said, "the selection of the *Greene* for this test provided an ideal sea trial situation by virtue of the lakes, rivers, locks and harbors which required the vessel to perform under a wide variety of operating conditions."

While refining shale oil currently is expensive, Horton expressed optimism that the new fuel would be competitive with conventional fuels when it is commercially produced.

He also stated there would be no reason why the 14-vessel Cleveland-Cliffs fleet could not switch to using the new fuel if the price were comparable to conventional fuels.

"Our tests showed that shale oil is equal to the design performance and reliability of conventional No. 6 oil," he said. "This was unexpected because our early studies of the new fuel indicated shale oil to be approximately 10 per cent lower in BTU content or thermal efficiency than No. 6 oil.

"We believe there is an important future for shale oil," he explained, "because this revolutionary test on the *Greene* has provided evidence that the new fuel can be used to operate a ship under all conditions."

Of course, economics will determine how extensively shale oil is used, but with demand for fuel continually expanding, especially in the processing, utility and maritime industries, shale oil could have a significant impact on the nation's energy requirements.

Testing the efficiency of shale oil as carrier fuel was carried out extensively during the run of the Cleveland Cliffs' Edward B. Greene. *(for full story see text)*

The Roger Blough.

8

The Modern Giants

A revolutionary change in Great Lakes vessels came about in 1971 with the development of the land-locked 1,000 ft. super-laker.

The *Stewart J. Cort* was the first of them. She became the largest vessel ever to transit the locks at Sault Ste. Marie, easing her 1,000 ft. x 105 ft. frame into the 1,100 x 110 ft. Poe Lock.

This first land locked super-laker is owned by the Great Lakes Steamship Division of Bethlehem Steel Corp. and on its maiden voyage from Erie to Taconite Harbor, Minnesota broke all previous records by carrying just short of 50,000 gross tons of taconite pellets for delivery to Bethlehem's mills at Burns Harbor, Indiana.

The *Cort* was constructed both in Mississippi and in Pennsylvania. Strange? Not really. The bow and stern were built by the Ingalls Shipbuilding Corporation at Pascagoula, Mississippi in 1970 and the mid-section by Erie Marine at Erie, Pa. in 1971. At Pascagoula, the bow and stern section of the ore carrier was built as one unit and launched that way. It was 182 feet long and sailed to Erie under its own steam, coming through the Seaway appropriately marked with a dotted line and the wry comment "cut here."

This "cutting" took place at Erie. The bow-stern section was cut apart and the 818-foot mid-body was virtually inserted at the Erie Marine mechanized ship assembly plant.

Powered by two twin propelled diesel engines of 14,000 HP, the *Cort* was the wonder of the Lakes, travelling at 10.5 knots fully loaded.

Designed to be the most efficient ore carrier in the system, she was the beginning of the present generation of self-unloading super carriers. The *Cort* carries a conveyor belt system which runs two lengths of her hull and can discharge up to 20,000[11] tons of taconite pellets per hour through her stern.

Twin bow thrusters as well as twin stern thrusters permit side maneuvering of the ship in constricted waters such as the rather severe turns of the St. Marys River. The bow thrusters consist of two straighthull five foot pipes extending through the sides of the bow and tightly affixed to the ship's outer pipes. Mounted inside the pipe is a propeller with a variable pitch blade which thrusts the water to the right or left of the vessel. Stern thrusters operate in the same manner.

A second super-laker came along shortly after the *Cort*. Although not quite as large, the U.S. Steel Corporation's *Roger Blough* was

[11]Most ore carriers backload with grain when they can. A vessel the size of the *Cort*—a super-laker—will carry 1,830,000 bushels of grain—the yield of 128 square miles of mid-continent prairie farm land. This amount of grain would produce 79,056,000 tons of flour or enough bread, laid end to end, to extend over four times the length of the United States at its widest point.

The Steward J. Cort, *first of the new generation of landlocked super-lakers.*

Two giants pass.

also land-locked at 858 feet—well over 125 ft. too long to ever transit the Seaway locks.

This self-unloading bulk carrier was completed by the American Shipbuilding Company at Lorain, Ohio, in 1972, and at the time was the largest vessel ever to be built entirely in the Great Lakes. Like the *Cort*, the *Blough's* bow is 105 feet beam but with a depth of 41 feet 6 inches rather than 49 feet.

At Lorain, work began first on the 437 ft. bow segment. Soon, simultaneous construction was started on the stern, at a new 1000 foot dry dock. The two halves of the vessel were joined in the dry dock.

At 858 feet the *Blough* seems dwarfed by the 1,000 foot vessel, but bear in mind that this $20 million U.S. Steel ore carrier is nearly the length of three football fields and has a carrying capacity of 45,000 gross tons. She can be unloaded at the rate of 10,000 tons per hour.

The *Blough* also carries double conveyor belts, running length-wise, which transfers taconite to an unloader mechanism at approximately 10,000 tons per hour.[12]

The vessel is run by a single 14,000 HP diesel with a single screw twenty feet in diameter, producing operating speeds of about 16.9 mph.

Each of the new vessels utilized some 16,000 tons of steel in construction.

In 1973, the *Cort* lost her position as the largest vessel on the Lakes when she was equaled by a tug-barge combination, the *Presque Isle* owned by Litton Industries and operated under charter to U.S. Steel. The *Presque Isle* equals both the carrying capacity and the length of the *Cort*.

This vessel operates on a unique principal and is known as an integrated tug-barge. Rather than being constructed as a single vessel, she is two. The after section contains the working parts of the vessel; everything other than the hold that is found on a conventional carrier has been designed into one section known as the "tug" portion of the vessel. The forward section, the hold, carries at its aft a v-shaped notch into which the tug fits snugly and is locked into place—hence the tug-barge integration.

The *Cort* and the *Presque Isle* were not long at the top of the list of Great Lakes giants. Soon, more than a half dozen 1,000 foot vessels were under construction at Great Lakes shipyards, including two more for Bethlehem Steel, three for Pickands Mather's Interlake fleet and one for GATX.

For the Pickands Mather vessels, power was installed in the form of two Colt-Pielstick engines designed and built by Colt Industries at Beloit, Wisc. The engines are of the PC-2 series for marine service, carrying a v-type configuration with sixteen cylinders, developing 500 BHT per cylinder at 520 RPM. Unique among engines, the Colt Pielstick needs less space and is lighter than other types of low speed steam propelled engines.

Each engine has an overall dimension of 27 feet by 11 feet, six inches and weighs about 150,000 pounds. Engine monitoring consoles are located both fore and aft, in the bridge and engine room to meet Coast Guard requirements (see diagram). Power is controlled directly from the bridge instead of the more conventional bridge-to-engine room telegraph system.

A substantial amount of the new vessel construction in the Lakes has been fostered by the 1970 Merchant Marine Act (see Chapter IX.) New traditions in design, safety and capacity emerged as the trend toward super-lakers and self-unloaders continues in the Lakes.

A new record for the largest vessel ever to be built entirely in the Lakes came about in late 1976 when the *James R. Barker* was launched. Expected to be the prototype of ore boats to come, the *Barker* also set a new Great Lakes cargo record—58,293 gross tons of taconite pellets—soon after she was launched. The vessel is operated by Pickands Mather and Company, a subsidiary of Moore McCormack Resources, Inc.

Built at Lorain, the *Barker* cost more than $40 million. She is 1,000 x 105 x 50, with a

---

[12]The *Cort*, also a modified self-unloader, uses a single belt under the cargo section, and transfers ore to a lifting wheel and then to an unloading mechanism located at the stern. This arrangement provides for an unloading capacity of 20,000 tons per hour.

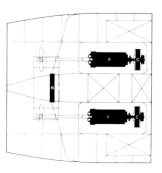

draft of 28 ft. Her cargo capacity is 59,000 gross tons of pellets or 52,000 net tons of coal. She has a discharge capacity of 10,000 long tons per hour with a self-unloader boom. Equipped with two diesel engines with 8,000 HP each, she cruises at 16 mph.

The *Barker* is double-hulled throughout, and all fuels, lubricants and sewage systems

(A) shows location of Colt-Pielstick engines, side view and from above for the Pickands Mather 1,000 foot super-carriers, (B) shows engine room control console and (C) reduction gearing.

The James R. Barker, *operated by the Inter-Lake Steamship Company, a Pickands Mather Division. The 1,000 foot × 105 foot vessel can carry 59,000 tons of taconite pellets or 52,000 tons of coal. Equipped with a 250 ft. self unloading boom, the* Barker *can discharge pellets at the rate of 10,000 tons per hour and coal at the rate of 6,000 tons per hour. The* Barker *is the first of two super-carriers to be built for Pickands Mather's inter-lake fleet by American Shipbuilding Company at Lorain.*

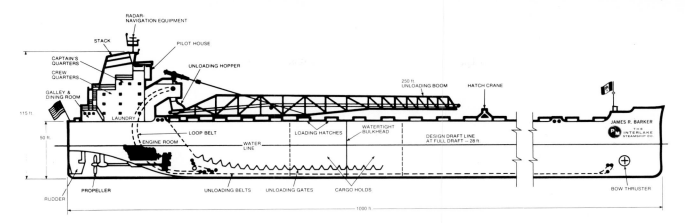

Side view of a super-laker – the James R. Barker.

are located within the inner hull. Nine ballast tanks are located along the sides of the ship, between the inner and outer hull sections. Each vertical tank has its own pumping system with no interconnected piping between tanks. This simplifies maintenance and provides a high degree of reliability.

The ballast tanks are flooded with water when the vessel is running without cargo to lower it in the water for increased maneuverability. The tanks are also kept flooded during loading operations to keep the deck hatches at the proper level of dockside loading equipment.

The huge cargo area is divided into seven holds. A series of power-actuated gates in each hold feeds pellets or coal onto three conveyor belts, running the length of the cargo hold area.

The three-belt unloading system is also effective for maximizing capacity when carrying coal.[13]

Main propulsion power for the *Barker* comes from two 8,000 HP diesel engines. Each engine is directly connected to a four-blade 17½ ft. diameter controllable-pitch propeller through a specially designed reduction gear and shafting system. To keep the drive systems simple but highly reliable, the four 800 KW, 480-volt main electrical generators are driven by separate diesel engines rather than off the main propulsion drive unit, as is the case in many other vessels.

Each controllable-pitch propeller assembly is fitted with four stainless steel movable blades. An automatic pitch-control system hydraulically changes propeller pitch according to engine speed to provide for optimum running economy and to prevent overloading and stalling the engines when heavily loaded at low speeds.

Maneuvering the huge 1,000-footer is simplified by the twin-screws and the arrangement of a rudder behind each propeller. The ship can also be steered by varying the speed of each engine. In addition, a 1,500 HP electrically driven bow thruster facilitates docking by pushing the bow to the right or left in much the same fashion as a tugboat.

Reversing is accomplished through controllable-pitch propellers; the engines do not reverse. This system greatly shortens the time it normally takes to generate a reverse response as compared with turbine-powered systems.

Due to the *Barker's* all-aft design and its overall height of 115 ft., a personnel elevator whisks crew members from the engine control-room level up the five decks to the level below the pilot house.

A 30-man crew is housed aft in modern, comfortably furnished quarters. Officers have

[13]Because of differing densities, a full load of coal will completely fill a hold, whereas a full load of pellets will not.

Inland Steel's new ore carrier the M.V. Joseph L. Block *is christened by the wife of the former Inland Chairman. The 31,000 ton self unloader will carry 2 million tons of ore annually to Inland's Indiana harbor works at East Chicago, Indiana, the nation's largest steel mill.*

single rooms and other crew members share a room. Crew quarters, the galley and engineer's control compartment are all air-conditioned.

An onboard sewage treatment plant produces clean effluent for discharge or for temporary holding while the vessel is in waters where discharge is prohibited by local regulations.

Pickands Mather has a sister ship to the *James R. Barker* now under construction.

Also in 1976 the *Joseph L. Block* joined the Inland Steel fleet. A self-unloader measuring 728 ft. in length, with a cargo capacity of 31,000 gross tons of ore, the vessel is not of the "super-laker" class. That is, she is not physically land-locked in the Great Lakes. She deserves mention here, however, because of innovative features which make her among the most sophisticated of the 700 ft.-class vessels in the Lakes.

The design of the *Block,* like that of the *Barker,* represents a departure from the traditional Great Lakes ore carrier with the pilot house forward and machinery aft. Its machinery, galley, crew quarters and pilot house are combined in a single four-deck structure aft.

Bay Shipbuilding Corp. built the *Block* at its Sturgeon Bay, Wisc. yard. The new vessel has a beam at 78 ft., a depth of 45 ft. and a draft of 27½ ft. when fully loaded. The 7,000 HP diesel engines give it a cruising speed of 15 mph.

The *Block* has the largest carrying capacity in Inland Steel's fleet of ore carriers. The *Block* joins the *SS Wilfred Sykes* as the second self-unloading vessel in Inland's fleet (the *Sykes* was converted to a self-unloader in 1975). This permits a six-hour unloading time.

This largest adddition to the fleet is required by the steel mill's increased need for

The Presque Isle, *integrated tug-barge leaves the Soo.*

Bow of a super-laker is launched.

Ready to accept a bow, this 660 foot section of a super-laker will also be fitted with a stern section to turn it, almost magically, into a super-laker.

This vessel under construction is the M/V Belle River *at Bay Shipbuilding Corporation.*

raw materials resulting from a current program to expand annual raw steel capacity by 2.1 million tons, or 24 percent, by the early 1980's.[14]

GATX Corp. has ordered two new carriers to be delivered to its subsidiary, American Steamship Co. of Buffalo, N.Y., one the 1,000 ft. super-laker mentioned previously. It is the first vessel of its size to be built at Bay Shipbuilding's Sturgeon Bay yards, and is being christened the *Belle River*.

The *Belle River* has a deadweight tonnage of 60,000 long tons, with an unloading capacity of 10,000 short tons of coal per hour. Her boom measures 250 ft. in length.

The other vessel built for American Steamship is a 634 ft. self-unloader with a capacity of 23,800 long tons of iron ore or 18,500 net tons of coal. She discharges cargo at a rate of 6,600 gross tons per hour. Diesel engines produce 7,000 HP and a cruising speed of 15.9 mph. Delivery is anticipated in mid-1978. The vessel will be a sister ship to American Steamship's *Sam Laud*, which entered service in May 1975.

The two new ships will bring the American Steamship fleet of self-unloaders to 20.

U. S. Steel has also contracted for two new super-lakers. The first 1,000 ft. ore carrier is expected to be completed in late 1978; the second is expected to be completed early in 1979. The 1,000 ft. self-unloaders will be 105 ft. wide and capable of carrying more than 58,000 long tons of iron ore pellets. Each will have a discharging rate of 10,000 gross tons of pellets per hour and more than 19,000 HP from two diesel engines.

[14]The added ore to support the new capacities will come from expansion of the Empire taconite mine and pellet plant at Palmer, Mich., of which Inland is part owner, and Inland's new Minorca Project at Virginia, Minn.

The super-laker H. Lee White.

Launching of a super-carrier section.

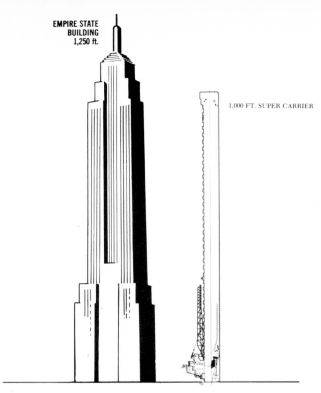

EMPIRE STATE
BUILDING
1,250 ft.

1,000 FT. SUPER CARRIER

1,000 ft. super-laker standing on end is almost as tall as Empire State Building.

Two new integrated tug-barges for Coordinated Caribbean Transport, Inc. of Miami, a subsidiary of Transway International Corp., New York, will add to the super-laker fleet. Built by Manhattan Barge, Inc., a subsidiary of Seatrain Shipbuilding Corp. of Brooklyn, New York, the barges carry a price tag of about $29 million. Twin tugs built in Marinette, Wisconsin by the Marinette Marine Corp., run the price up an added $14 million.

These vessels are known as ARTUBAR ships, articulated tug-barges. The tug and barge are connected by means of pins jutting out of either side of the tug's bow. The pins fit into sockets in the recessed stern of the barge. They can rotate in the sockets, allowing the tug to pitch relative to the barge. As an added safety feature, these pins can also retract rapidly so that the tug and barge can disconnect quickly when necessary.

Known as stubby, this bow-hull combination moves through the St. Lawrence Seaway, never to return again. Cut apart at American Shipbuilding at Lorain, the 'ship' became the Stewart J. Cort; *the first 1,000 footer to sail as a landlocked super-laker.*

140

Zip 48222

Zip 48222 is the postal code assigned to the *J.W. Westcott II*, a 45 ft. vessel that serves the Great Lakes fleet as mailman. The vessel delivers mail to the ships that move through the Lakes and the Detroit River.

For a number of years, the U.S. Post Office has declined to enter into more than a year-to-year contract with the *Westcott*, and upon several occasions considered terminating the vessels' service. Each threat was met with such protests by the Great Lakes carriers that the service was continued.

The *Westcott* has been hauling mail — including laundry and personal messages — since 1948. The ship operates 24 hours a day, as long as traffic moves through the system.

The Westcott Company was formed in 1874 by Captain J.W. Westcott; it is headed today by Joseph J. Hogan.

The Canadian Steamship vessel Frontenac.

The Soo River Company's George G. Henderson.

The 700-ft. Cliffs Victory *passing Detroit.*

9

The Impact of Legislation

The single most important piece of legislation to involve the Great Lakes since the Wiley-Dondero Act created the Seaway in 1959, was the passage of the 1970 Amendments to the Merchant Marine Act of 1936. That Act, to be known as the Merchant Marine Act of 1970, emerged from a House-Senate Joint Committee with amendments of critical importance to the System. It made the Great Lakes a fourth seacoast for the United States. And, it was to become precursor of a new and revitalized Great Lakes marine.

Traditionally, the United States had been divided into three maritime areas, all of them tidewater. The Atlantic and Pacific seaboards, and the region surrounding the Gulf of Mexico had, until 1970, defined the traditional American seacoasts—east, west and gulf, and it was among these three regions that a full hundred percent of the federal benefits accruing to the maritime industry were divided. The vast multi-billion maritime industry of the Great Lakes region existed without the advantages of federal support and indeed, found its own tax dollars used against itself by tidewater competitors.

The inequity to which the Great Lakes addressed itself was voiced often, but of no avail, until convening of the 1970 hearings of the House Merchant Marine and Fisheries

Committee and the Senate Committee on Commerce.

At these hearings, two groups came forth to champion the cause of the system. The Great Lakes Task Force, under the chairmanship of the redoubtable Louis C. Purdey, and the Great Lakes Commission, represented by its executive director, Col. Leonard J. Goodsell. Purdey, then Executive Director of the Toledo-Lucas County Port Authority, and at the time President of the National Waterways Conference, was also chairman of the Commission's Seaway Commerce and Navigation Committee.

The Great Lakes Task Force had as its membership, The Council of Lake Erie Ports, The Great Lakes Commission, The Great Lakes Terminals Association, The International Association of Great Lakes Ports (U.S. Section) The International Longshoremen's Association (Great Lakes District) and The U.S. Great Lakes Shipping Association.

The Commission is a compact agency founded to represent the water resources interests of the eight states which surround the Great Lakes. The commission told both the House and Senate committees that, "In updating the Merchant Marine Act of 1936, we request that two major objectives be met for the Great Lakes: First, recognize the Great Lakes region as the fourth seacoast of the Un-

Discussing Great Lakes shipping from left are: Robert J. Blackwell, Asst. Secretary of Commerce in charge of Maritime Affairs; David W. Oberlin, Administrator of the St. Lawrence Seaway Development Corporation which controls the U.S. section of the Seaway; Retired Congressman John Blatnik, former Chairman of the Public Works Committee. Blatnik's efforts were immensely significant in the ultimate construction of the Seaway. Oberlin has pushed the system to record tonnage levels and Blackwell, as head of the U.S. Maritime Administration, is responsible for operating and construction subsidies of vessels in the Great Lakes, as well as loan guarantees.

ited States and include the Great Lakes port range with the Atlantic, Gulf and Pacific port ranges and secondly, provide for the replacement and modernization of our Great Lakes fleet."

The House version of the bill was passed without the inclusion of the Great Lakes into the Federal government's maritime subsidy program. The House did not vote to give coastal status to the Great Lakes. The Senate, however, did include provisions recommended by the Task Force and the Commission, and, as a result, the Merchant Marine legislation went into Joint Committee to hammer out compromise legislation.

The emerging legislation, to the immense relief and gratification of the entire system, included the Great Lakes and the nation's Fourth Seacoast was born.

Another amendment to the Act granted to the St. Lawrence Seaway Development Corporation the forgiveness of interest on the Seaway's construction debt, enabling SLSDC — the agency charged with the operation of the U.S. Seaway — to begin a realistic repayment plan which would ultimately eliminate that debt entirely.

The amendments which created the Fourth Seacoast provided the Great Lakes domestic shipping industry for the first time with tax deferral privileges and incentives, construction loan guarantees, and operating and construction differential subsidies.

The Lakes also qualified for a range of studies and related assistance efforts. By vir-

tue of the fact that the Act had as its purpose to attract U.S. Flag shipping to the Fourth Seacoast, the Lakes ports could now benefit from Federal Cargo Preference programs.

When the Act was signed into law, the bonded debt of the Seaway Corporation—the cost of the construction of the St. Lawrence Seaway—stood at $159.2 million. Since the opening of the Seaway in 1959, SLSDC had paid over $37.6 million against the debt—but all of that money had been applied to interest payments, and none to the principal.

Seaway Administrator D.W. Oberlin called the interest-eliminating legislation a "practical, expedient method of dealing with a problem of considerable proportion" for the Seaway-Great Lakes system.

He said that the bill "relieves the pressure for higher tolls, which, in and of itself, would have created adverse effect upon the mid-continent and upon dozens of Great Lakes ports.

Then-GOP Whip Sen. Robert P. Griffin, one of five senators chosen to iron out differences between House and Senate versions of the Act, said at that time that the legislative action would "relieve mounting pressure to increased tolls which, if put into effect, would further reduce shipping traffic in the Seaway."

Althouth Great Lakes operators in the international trade had always been eligible for Construction Differential Subsidy and Operating Differential Subsidy, at the time the Merchant Marine Act of 1970 was written,

One of many groups meeting to deal with Great Lakes shipping activities. A highly cohesive and interested maritime community exists in the system.

no U.S.-built ships with or without subsidy were serving the Great Lakes international trade.

The immediate effect of the passage of the legislation for the Seway was to eliminate $25.7 million in deferred interest charges which had accrued since the 1959 opening of the Seaway. And that $25.7 million was above the $37.6 million in interest which had been paid by the Seaway Corporation from its toll income between 1959 and 1969.

Oberlin notes that, "The legislation has allowed SLSDC to pay $15 million in toll income over the last five years on the original Seaway construction debt, thus reducing that amount to $118.5 million, as of now."

What would have happened had the Merchant Marine Act not been passed? "First," he comments, "our bonded debt would have remained at $133.5 million. Second, our deferred interest due, plus interest accrued between 1970-75, would have added on $62.7 million. Even subtracting the $15 million we have paid on the revenue bonds since 1970, the SLSDC total bonded and interest debt as of now would have been $181.2 million instead of just the $118.5 million total now remaining.

"Third, without the Act, we would undoubtedly have had to raise Seaway tolls, which have remained unchanged since 1959, and this, of course, would have cost American consumers more for the commodities being shipped via the Seaway.

"In a nutshell, the Act saved extra costs to the consumer and spared the Seaway Corporation $62.7 million in interest payments."

Substantial vessel-oriented benefits have accrued to the Great Lakes as a result of the legislation. Since the Act was signed into law:

— Construction Subsidy applications have been made by four major Great Lakes-Seaway operators.
— $263,000,000 in Title XI loans have been guaranteed in the Great Lakes for the construction of 11 vessels, such as the *Presque Isle, James R. Barker* and *William Roesch,* along with ten deck barges. Applications are pending now for $161,000,000 more for Great Lakes vessel construction.
— Twenty-four Great Lakes-Seaway operators have established capital construction funds in excess of $645,000,000. These funds have made possible the acquisition or reconstruction of a resounding 71 vessels including 14 tugs and barges.
— Operating Subsidies have been applied to two major lines in the Great Lakes, two others qualify on incentive or privilege calls and others are readying applications.

What did all this mean in terms of an improved economic climate for the Great Lakes? Primarily, benefits in four areas: Construction Differential Subsidies, Title XI Loan Guarantees, Tax Deferral Privileges and Operating Differential Subsidies.

An important aspect of the Merchant Marine Act amendments for the Great Lakes was the Construction Differential Subsidy (CDS). The CDS program represents the difference in cost between a ship constructed in a foreign shipyard and the same ship built in a U.S. shipyard. Due to the cost differential, a Federal subsidy is necessary to place the construction costs of ships built in the United States on a parity with foreign construction costs.

The purpose of the subsidy is to encourage the growth and maintenance of both the U.S. merchant marine and the U.S. shipbuilding industry, and to thereby insure a degree of national self-sufficiency in these industries.

CDS may also be paid to aid in the reconstruction and reconditioning of existing ships.

The Great Lakes shipbuilding industry has traditionally looked inward to the domestic fleet owners for their business. With the opening of the Seaway and the Congressional support for the Fourth Seacoast, some Great Lakes shipbuilders have now expressed interest in the Construction Differential Subsidy programs available for ships which are to compete in an international trade on prescribed subsidized trade routes.

In order to encourage the Department of Commerce's Maritime Administration to give equal consideration to the shipyards on the Fourth Seacoast, the 94th Congress on November 13, 1975 amended the Merchant Marine Act of 1970 to require that not less than 10% of the funds appropriated for Construction and Operating Subsidy be allocated to each port range provided that approved applications had been submitted.

In September 1976, the first Construction Subsidy was awarded to a Great Lakes shipyard when Marinette Marine Corporation was awarded a contract to build two tug vessels for Coordinated Caribbean Transport. These tugs will become part of an integrated tug/barge system which will operate in service between Miami and Central America ports. These tugs, to be built in Marinette, Wisconsin, are estimated to cost $13,757,000.

Loan Guarantees under Title XI of the Merchant Marine Act appear to be one of the most widely used financial aid programs by the Great Lakes maritime community. The guarantees are applicable to just about every kind of American built vessel above a minimum size, provided the project and owners seem to be economically viable.

The Federal Ship Financing Program, established under Title XI, provides for a guarantee by the federal government of debt obligations issued by citizen shipowners for the purpose of financing or refinancing flag vessels constructed or reconstructed in shipyards.

Vessels built with Construction Differential Subsidy or vessels other than barges and passenger vessels, engaged solely in the transportation of property on inland rivers and canals, exclusively, are eligible only for a guarantee not exceeding 75 percent.

Secretary of Transportation Brock Adams (right) and Seaway Administrator David W. Oberlin. His colleagues in the Senate have predicted that Secretary Adams, a former Washington congressman, would become the greatest Secretary of Transportation in the nation's history. He is the country's sixth DOT Secretary; Oberlin is the fourth and the strongest Administrator the Seaway has seen since it opened the Great Lakes to world commerce in 1959.

Seaway Administrator D. W. Oberlin (right) with familiar Seaway supporter, Vice President Walter Mondale. As a U.S. Senator, the Vice President introduced and supported much legislation vital to the Seaway-Great Lakes system.

Lake Carriers' President Vice Admiral Paul E. Trimble (USCG Ret.), right, with Michigan Governor William G. Milliken and Ontario Premier William Davies.

Dominion Marine's Rear Admiral (Ret.) Robert W. Timbrell.

Great Lakes vessels constructed under Title XI guarantees include the Paul Thayer (bottom left), Presque Isle (top center), James R. Barker (top right), H. Lee White (lower right), Charles E. Wilson (lower center) and William Roesch (upper left). Title XI construction guarantees became possible when, finally, the Merchant Marine Act of 1970 gave seacoast status to Great Lakes. Complete list of Title XI vessels through 1976 appears on page 151.

The guarantee generally increases the ability of a firm to raise long-term capital at reasonable rates to be about equal to triple-A industrials.

Since the Federal Ship Financing Program is a guarantee program and not a direct loan program, funds secured by the guaranteed debt obligations and used for the financing of vessels are obtained in the private sector. The main sources for such funds include banks, pension trusts, life insurance companies and bonds sold to the general public.

A revolving fund of $7 billion facilitates the debt financing available to the Great Lakes shipowners.

In 1976, Title XI applications pending for Great Lakes vessels were valued at more than $158 million.

Assistant Secretary of Commerce for Maritime Affairs, Robert J. Blackwell has called the Title XI program, "one of the most valuable resources available to Great Lakes operators."

"Such guarantees" he has noted, "are currently in force for the construction of 11 bulk carriers, one tug/barge unit, 10 deck barges, and the reconstruction of a bulk carrier.

"These projects have a combined total value of $263 million. In addition, we have Title XI applications pending for an additional $158 million in Great Lakes vessel construction."

Fighters for the Fourth Seacoast legislation in both the Congress and the Executive branch of government are all smiles after the passage of the legislation. Shown left to right are Seaway Administrator D. W. Oberlin, Michigan Senators Robert P. Griffin and Philip A. Hart, Rep. John A. Blatnik, Minn., John A. Volpe, former Secretary of Transportation, Rep. Ancher Nelson, Minn., and John D. Dingell, Mich.

Vessels built since 1973 under Title XI guarantees include the following:

Vessel	Owner	Builder	Estimated Cost
1973			
Charles E. Wilson 25,000 dwt.	Franklin Steamship Co.	Bay Ship-building Corp.	$13.7 million
William Roesch *Paul Thayer* 19,000 dwt. each	Kinsman Marine Transit Co.	American Shipbuilding Co.	$12.4 million $12.6 million
Roger M. Kyes 25,000 dwt.	Edison Steamship Co.	American Shipbuilding Co.	$14 million
Presque Isle G.L. tug/barge 57,500 dwt.	Litton Industries Leasing Corp.	Halter Marine Service	$35 million
1974			
H. Lee White 25,000 dwt.	Fulton Steamship Co.	Bay Ship-building Corp.	$14.3 million
Wolverine 19,000 dwt.	Oglebay Norton Co.	American Shipbuilding Co.	$14.1 million
1975			
James R. Barker *Hull No. 906* 59,000 dwt. each	Interlake Steamship Co.	Halter Marine Service	$43.4 million $45.1 million
Sam Laud 23,300 dwt.	Whitney Steamship Co.	Bay Ship-building Corp.	$13.3 million
1976			
MV St. Clair 42,000 dwt.	Bell Steamship Co.	Bay Ship-building Corp.	$24.3 million
Herbert Jackson 25,000 dwt.	Interlake Steamship Co.	Defoe Ship-building Co.	$6.1 million (Reconstruction)
10 deck barges	Bultema Dock and Dredge Co.	Maxon Marine Ind. Twin City Shipyard	$2.8 million

Another valuable form of financial assistance available to Great Lakes ship operators under the Act is the Capital Construction Fund program. Tax-deferred revenues and income may be deposited in such funds to enable operators to accumulate capital needed for vessel replacement or modernization, that is, acquisitions, construction, or reconstruction.

In 1976, 24 Great Lakes operators established such funds for the construction or acquisition of vessels valued in excess of $645 million.

The Capital Construction Fund (CCF) program was created by the 1970 amendments as a method of helping operators accumulate necessary capital for the modernization and expansion of the merchant marine.

The program is available to all American flag operators operating vessels in the U.S., foreign, Great Lakes, and non-contiguous domestic commerce, or in the fisheries of the United States.

CCF provides for the deferment of federal income taxes on earnings or gains realized from the operation of agreement vessels, proceeds from the sale of an agreement vessel or from insurance or compensation from the loss of an agreement vessel.

The Fund is a mechanism to permit American flag operators to compete more favorably with the non-American flag operators who use the benefit of tax havens outside the U.S. in order to shelter their income.

The intent of the Fund is to encourage U.S. flag operators to modernize and expand their fleets, while promoting the construction of ships in U.S. shipyards.

Ship operating subsidies are available to encourage and assist American flag operators to compete in the Great Lakes foreign trades.

The Operating Differential Subsidy (ODS) program in the Great Lakes today rather exclusively applies to Lykes Bros. and Farrell Lines.

Traditionally, Great Lakes overseas shipping services have been dominated by non-U.S. flag, non-conference carriers.

This fact has made it difficult for U.S. flag service to compete on a break-bulk service from the Great Lakes.

Ships eligible for the ODS program include all modern types of cargo carrying ships (barge carriers, containerships, roll-on/roll-off vessels, tankers, ore/bulk/oil carriers, etc.) whose designs are satisfactory to the United States or commercial operation in an essential foreign trade. Such ships must be built in the United States, controlled by citizens of the United States and manned with United States citizen crews.[15]

What about operational subsidies for the Great Lakes domestic fleet? The Act prohibits the payment of ODS to any person or company engaged either directly or indirectly in domestic trade, unless the government, after a hearing in those cases where proper interventions are filed, specifically permits domestic operation. An exception is provided if the ODS contractor, or a related person or firm, was in bona fide operation as a common carrier by water in the domestic trade in 1935.

Congress provided additional assistance to the Fourth Seacoast in February 1975 when it amended the Merchant Marine Act of 1970 to require the Maritime Administration to open a regional office in each of the four port ranges.

Since the other coasts already had region offices, it was clear their intention was for MarAd to open an office on the Great Lakes. On June 5, 1975, following a Great Lakes Commission survey of Great Lakes interests, Blackwell announced that the new Great Lakes Region office would be located in Cleveland, Ohio in order to insure a broad range of MarAd's services to the Great Lakes maritime community.

"Establishment of these offices," he noted, "is consistent with the course of the Merchant Marine Act of 1970 which recognized the Great Lakes as the nation's Fourth Seacoast."

[15]Federal Subsidies are available, also, for certain types of passenger vessels, but there are no pending applications for assistance for either construction or operation of such vessels on the Great Lakes. While some Great Lakes states have expressed an interest in passenger travel incidental to cargo movements on car or train ferries, other states have expressed an interest in tourist passenger travel by fast vessels during a limited period of the summer season. Still, it is not anticipated that federal assistance will be sought.

The Region Office has been open since November 5, 1975, and has a staff of 15 people in four Great Lakes cities. The major programs include Ports and Intermodal Systems, Ship Management and Market Development.

The future of the Great Lakes with the advent of the Merchant Marine Act amendments, is "full steam ahead" says George Ryan, who heads MarAd's Great Lakes Region Office.

"We see a future for the Great Lakes which includes sharp increases in cargo moved in our domestic, U.S./Canada and international trades. This means increases not only in the Great Lakes participation in MarAd's financial programs, but also increased participation in our Construction and Operating Subsidy programs."

What does it all mean? More jobs, certainly, and better port utilization. More economical vessel utilization. A newer, revitalized fleet. A stronger climate for the development of the Great Lakes states, and a vastly expanded utilization of one of the nation's major transportation arteries.

Lake carrier as seen at low water in the Seaway lock while two others wait on the wall.

Huletts work ore carrier.

Aspirations Toward Regional Transportation Planning: The Great Lakes Basin Commission

The Great Lakes Basin Commission (GLBC) was established by Presidential Executive Order in 1967 to coordinate and promote regional planning in the Great Lakes region. The Commission, not to be confused with the Great Lakes Commission, (an eight-state compact agency) serves the constituent states in an advisory capacity, including analysis and dissemination of information with respect to water and land resources, coastal management and transportation.

In recognition of the importance of this latter area, GLBC formed a Standing Committee on Transportation, chaired by Coast Guard Rear Admiral James S. Gracey, with membership consisting of a number of authorities on Great Lakes transportation. The purpose of the Committee is the discussion of important policy issues, such as port development, in Great Lakes transportation. Although most attention has concentrated on maritime transportation, it is the intention of the GLBC Committee to provide a forum to discuss other modes, intermodalism, and regionalism in Great Lakes transportation.

The Standing Committee has presented a series of workshops on specific topics related to transportation. All of these activities stem from the Commission's concern with regionalism in transportation. As new issues and ideas develop, GLBC intends to consider them, not necessarily with the intention of developing solutions, but rather (perhaps more correctly) with the intention of stimulating relevant thought.

Upbound and downbound ore boats pass in ice.

10

Breaking the Ice Barrier

In winter months, roughly between mid-December and early April, the Great Lakes closes down, or to put it more properly, the Lakes are closed down by winter and by the ice that clogs its rivers, its channels and its ports.

The dynamic, vigorous transportation system known throughout the world, the Fourth Seacoast of the United States and the southern coast of Canada, is out of business. The great ports, with their giant gantries and cargo-moving apparatus are stilled. The docks are silent and the slips are glazed over with many feet of ice. The ore boats head for safe moorings to wait out the weather. Commerce stops.

The dilemma of an eight month shipping season has plagued the Great Lakes since the days of sail. Because ice does close down shipping, industries relying upon water transportation for the cartage of their cargoes are forced to stock-pile to carry them through the winter months, or, alternatively, to have materials shipped overland at immensely higher rates. The system would obviously be more efficient if it could operate year round or at least for a longer period of time.

Great Lakes shipping is an obviously indisputable link in the industrial and agricultural economy of the mid-continent. When we consider that the eight Great Lakes states contain 26% of the nations' population and 80% of the population classified as urban; is responsible for 36% of the nations' value-added-through manufacturing; 47% of the nations'

steel production (as well, the Great Lakes hinterland produces 80% of the raw materials required for steel production in the U.S.); 12% of the nations' mining (71% of the nations' iron ore and 40% of its limestone) and 37% of the nations' grain, it becomes abundantly clear how dependent the Great Lakes states are on low-cost water transportation.

An investigation into the possibility of extending the navigation season on the Great Lakes and in the St. Lawrence Seaway came about in 1970 as a result of an amendment (Section 107) to the Rivers and Harbors Act of that year. With this legislation, Congress authorized the expenditure of an initial $6.5 million over a three year period to see if it was feasible and economically beneficial to extend the season on the Lakes.

Without getting into the technicalities of the Act, it is sufficient to say that the effort has been immensely successful. In the 1974 shipping season, in fact, the upper four Great Lakes—those dealing mightily in the dry bulk trades and used so extensively by lake carriers—remained open year round.

The Federal demonstration program has called for ship voyages extending beyond the normal navigation season, for the observation of ice conditions and ice forces, environmental and ecological investigation, collections of technical data relating to improved vessel design, ice control facilities, navigation aids and a collection and dissemination of information to shippers on weather and ice conditions.

Unique aerial shows ore carriers making their way toward open water.

In order to accomplish the objectives established by Congress, a Winter Navigation Board was established to oversee the program, chaired by the U.S. Army Corps of Engineers. The board consists of leadership of the U.S. Coast Guard (Vice Chairman), The St. Lawrence Seaway Development Corporation, The National Oceanic and Atmospheric Administration, U.S. Maritime Administration, U.S. Department of the Interior, Environmental Protection Agency, The Federal Power Commission, The Great Lakes Basin Commission, and The Great Lakes Commission. Technical advisors of the program include the National Aeronautics and Space Administration and the Atomic Energy Commission, now known as the National Energy Administration. Canadian observers as well as labor and industrial leaders were invited to participate in the program.

The investigation to date has concluded that the extension of the shipping season in the system is, indeed, feasible from an engineering standpoint and can produce immense economic benefits for the Great Lakes region and for the nation as a whole, with little or no adverse effects on the environment.

The Federal government looks at such projects in terms of a benefit-cost ratio. This means that return of a given number of dollars might be expected out of the expenditure of a given sum of money. In other words, a benefit-cost ratio (B/C) of 3/1 would mean that three dollars of benefit would be returned for every one dollar spent.

Among the specific and more obvious areas from which savings could be generated by an extended season is the fact that it would be no longer necessary to winter stock-pile bulk commodities. This, of course, would release the capital represented by stock-pile inventory and real estate which are now necessary.

Another obvious area of savings is to be found in the more efficient utilization of the Great Lakes fleet—an extended season would automatically facilitate the use of newer and more efficient vessels over a longer period of time, as well as result in further investments in new vessels. The expansion and modernization of the merchant marine in the Great Lakes, experts say, would occur virtually automatically as the result of an extended season.

Other benefits accruing from year-round navigation were spelled out before the House Committee on Public Works and the Transportation Sub-committee on Water Resources by Great Lakes interests, including the Great Lakes Task Force and Great Lakes Commission, which quoted the U.S. Dept. of Commerce in noting that a 12 month navigation season would provide 42,000 jobs in the 11 states that comprise the immediate Great Lakes economic region.

This would mean an estimated $382,000,000 in additional labor earnings generated through 1980 (1967 dollars). As well, the year-round season would bring stability of the Great Lakes labor force.

Operational measures necessary for implementation of the program and for the expansion of the winter navigation effort include:
— Increased icebreaking capability.
— Improved navigational aids.
— Ice and weather forecasting operations and data collection.
— Ice monitoring programs.
— Year-round lock operations.
— Operation of vehicles to allow the residents of islands in constricted channels to get to shore.

Winter navigation

Some familiar leaders in the winter navigation effort: standing—David W. Oberlin, Administrator of the U.S. St. Lawrence Seaway; Brig. Gen. Robert L. Moore, Division Engineer, North Central Division which is responsible for the Great Lakes; seated—Rear Admiral James S. Gracey, former Commandant, Ninth Coast Guard District, and now U.S.C.G. Chief of Staff and Congressman Philip Ruppe (R-Mich.) ranking minority leader of the House Merchant Marine and Fisheries Committee and a strong and articulate friend of the Great Lakes.

Portion of Winter Navigation Board leadership at recent meeting. From left, NOAA's Rear Adm. Harley D. Nygren; Maritime Administration's George Ryan; Vice-Chairman of the Board, Rear Adm. James S. Gracey, U.S. Coast Guard; Board Chairman, Brig, Gen. Robert J. Moore, Corps of Engineers; St. Lawrence Seaway Development Corp. Administrator, David W. Oberlin, and Ms. Madonna McGrath, Special Assistant to the Secretary of the Interior. In foreground, back to camera, is Canadian observer, Allan Luce.

Union concern over the safety and well-being of seamen must be comforting at a time like this.

U.S. Steel vessel at Straits of Mackinac.

Also, in order to assure year-round navigation, permanent structures must be installed at Sault Ste. Marie and tested under severe ice conditions. Problems at the Mackinac Straits, the St. Clair Channel, the Welland and St. Lawrence Canals and locks must also be addressed and solved. In terms of the Seaway itself, problems are more than of an engineering nature, but include complex legal issues that must be defined and dealt with, perhaps on a Department of State level.

There are a number of tangible benefits that have already resulted from the Demonstration Program. For instance, Sault Ste. Marie has already been kept open year-around. The number of transits through the Soo after December 15, 1974 increased from 40 carrying 400,000 tons for the year previous, to 776 transits carrying 9.1 million tons.

The additional tonnage shipped as a result of an extended navigation season—between the 15th of December and the 31st of March—can be seen in the chart below. Showing the years 1972, 1973 and 1974 respectively, the chart shows millions of tons shipped during a period when shipping would normally be closed down because of ice. Points of origin for the bulk commodity cargoes are Lakes Superior, Michigan, Huron, Erie, Ontario and the St. Clair and Detroit Rivers. During those three years, nearly 21 million tons of cargo were shipped, which would otherwise not have been shipped.

Taconite pellets – a great deal of what winter navigation is all about.

Duluth looks cold as a winter storm sets in.

Snow storm on the Lakes.

Great Lakes Commercial Shipping: Extended Navigation Season

(Millions of Tons Shipped)

Commodity	1972	1973	1974	1975
Iron Ore	1.17	3.90	4.93	8.39
Grain	0.71	0.62	1.10	1.70
Coal	1.13	0.67	1.65	2.20
Stone	0.14	0.49	1.12	1.10
Petroleum	0.37	0.76	0.98	1.00
Other	0.06	0.29	0.85	0.51

The benefits which can occur in the St. Lawrence Seaway as a result of an extended season is shown in the chart below. Traffic for the total system is taken into account for three alternative extensions of the season—one to January 31, a second to February 28 and a third year-round. It is interesting to note that the benefits of a year-round system operation in 1975 would return 68 million dollars, while in just 50 years that figure would soar to 247 million.

Benefits to the Great Lakes-St. Lawrence Seaway System From Season Extension

Year	January 31	February 28	Year-Round
1975	$ 40,283,000	$ 58,593,000	$ 68,223,000
1985	85,205,000	123,934,000	140,824,000
2005	119,091,000	173,223,000	196,555,000
2025	150,674,000	219,162,000	247,381,000

Coast Guard cutter helps carrier J.L. Mathe. *Note track at aft of carrier.*

Ice.

Extension of the inter-lake shipping season has been met with mixed feelings by labor. Mel Pelfrey, Vice President of the National Marine Engineers Beneficial Association, District 2 (*MEBA*) has noted that while labor is not opposed to an extended season, it recognizes that there are serious human problems that must be solved before labor can give its whole-hearted endorsement to the effort.

"Labor is primarily concerned with the human factors that must be solved before the winter demonstration program becomes old hat and dangerous," says Pelfrey. "And the unacceptable risks become commonplace.

"So far we have been lucky, but we don't want to have to convene a board of inquiry to determine what happened to one of our ships, and most importantly, one of its crews as a result of winter navigation."

One of labor's concerns is that for all practical purposes, inter-lake traffic in iron ore may have already grown out of the demonstration stage and into a full competitive stage.

To maritime labor this represents a dangerous trend. "I can see every shipping company in the Great Lakes being forced to put ships in the winter navigation season—ships that are unsuitable for navigation in ice and cold weather," Pelfrey says.

The extension of presently restricted shipping is of critical importance to the nation in its efforts to expand capacities of our natural transportation network and, at the same time, reduce transportation cost and reserve transportation fuels. What is necessary for the realization of the potential of a more adequate shipping season for the Great Lakes?

Federal agencies involved in the effort to expand the season should take immediate steps to implement programs which have been successfully demonstrated. The Coast Guard should step up planning for the replacement of obsolecent general purpose tugs with vessels with greater icebreaking capacity. This, as a matter of fact, is being done with the construction of five new icebreaking tugs for the Coast Guard.

Congressional support is necessary for a permanent extension of the navigation season on the four upper lakes where year-round shipping has proved itself realistic, profitable and feasible. Finally, an intensification of effort should take place for the development of an extended season for the balance of the system—The Lake Ontario and St. Lawrence River system in concert with the government of Canada.

This, of course, is necessary so that the entire system might achieve at some early future date, an extended navigation season. The Demonstration Program has proved the feasibility and the economic benefits of an extended navigation season on the Great Lakes. The national interest now requires that the nation move forward to implement the results of the study and to provide the funds necessary to make an extended navigation season truly a reality.

Fuel Conservation Puts the Great Lakes in the Lead

The Winter Navigation Board's Interim Report on an Extended Navigation Season forecasts the movement of 15 million gross tons (GT) of iron ore from the Head-of-the-Lakes area to lower Lake Michigan during an extended (year-round) season.

A comparison of capabilities of this kind of cargo movement by three transportation modes—water, rail and truck, indicates this:

	Water	Rail	Truck
Single unit trip capacity (GT)	50,000	6,500	25
Units required to deliver 15 million GT	300	2,308	600,394

A rail unit is here defined as a train consisting of one hundred 65GT capacity freight cars with four locomotives. In this example, 217.7 trains, so defined, are required.

A truck unit is defined as a dual or tandem-axle truck with trailer.

For the movement of the 15 million GT of iron ore, the water route distance is 800 miles, the rail route is 465 miles and the highway route, 490 miles. Ton-miles compute, on this basis, 12 billion ton/miles for highway movement.

Fuel consumption, computed on a ton/mile-gallon basis is as follows:

	Water	Rail	Truck
Ton/miles per gallon of fuel	500	200	60
Fuel consumption for transporting 15 million tons of iron ore	24 million gallons	35 million gallons	123 million gallons

A savings of 11 million gallons of fuel is effected through the use of water, rather than rail shipment, and nearly 100 million gallons of fuel are saved in shipping by water rather than by highway.

The impact of this kind of savings in an energy shortage should be obvious. The reduced impact on the environment in terms of air pollution should be equally clear.

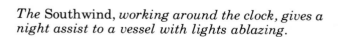

The Southwind, *working around the clock, gives a night assist to a vessel with lights ablazing.*

The 290 foot icebreaker Mackinaw.

The Coast Guard in Winter

The Coast Guard plays a very visible role in the Demonstration Program. Two large icebreakers, the *Mackinaw,* (especially built for Great Lakes service) and the polar classed *Westwind*, plus smaller ice-strengthened vessels, have been deployed to rivers and constricted channels to maintain a flow of traffic during the program. Three regular Coast Guard operations have traditionally moved into gear when the winter freeze occurs. These are in Coast Guard jargon, operations "taconite," "coal shovel," and "oil can," supporting the trades suggested by their names.

Under the direction of the Sault Ste. Marie Coast Guard group, icebreaking for the *taconite* operation centers itself in the Whitefish Bay—St. Marys River—Straits of Mackinac area. Here the 290 foot *Mackinaw,* and the *Westwind* keep shipping ice open for ore boats carrying taconite from Two Harbors, Minnesota to the mills of Gary and Chicago. They normally are assisted by the 180 foot *Woodrush*, out of Duluth and the 110 foot *Naugatuck* and *Arundel* from the Soo along with the *Sundew* out of Charlevoix.

Operation coal shovel works to insure the uninterrupted movement of coal from southern Lake Erie—primarily Toledo, to plants and factories in the Detroit area. Icebreaker assistance comes from small vessels, the *Acacia*, the *Caw*, the *Ojibwa* and the *Mariposa. Oil can* involves cutters *Muskeet* out of Sturgeon Bay and *Raritan* from Grand Haven. This operation assists tankers in the Grand Traverse Bay and other parts of the northern Lakes region.

The air cushion vehicle icebreaker, ICEATER as she prepares for tests by the Canadian Coast Guard in frozen Great Lakes waters. The ICEATER has earned a reputation of being, conceptually, one of the most ingenious icebreaking machines ever devised.

One of the smaller Coast Guard units which work with ships in ice. This one is the cutter Ojibwa.

Carrier falls into track cut in ice by icebreaker.

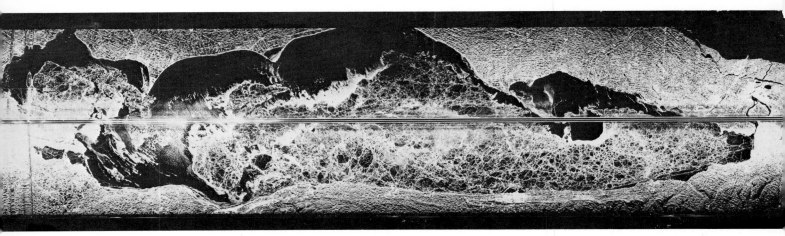

SLAR photo of Lake Erie. Line in center is flight line of aircraft. Comparable map shown in inset.

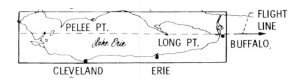

Fighting Ice With SLAR

A system for monitoring ice conditions on the Great Lakes and providing near-real time information about ice location, type and thickness directly to the ships' bridges for winter navigation has been developed at the NASA Lewis Research Center.

At the heart of the system are two major aircraft-mounted components: a side-looking airborne radar (SLAR) system, for detecting ice cover and type, and a modified short-pulse S-band radar system for simultaneously determining ice thickness, regardless of cloud cover.

As the aircraft flies over the approximate center-line of the body of water, the ice data are taken as continuing (analog) data. The data are digitized and sent by radio transmission either directly or via NOAA satellite to a ground receiving station.

From the receiving station, the data are sent via landlines (telephone) to the U.S. Coast Guard Ice Navigation Center at Cleveland, Ohio. The data on ice cover, type and thickness are used to produce an annotated map. The map together with the SLAR image are sent via landlines to the Marine Radio Telephone Transmitter at Lorain, Ohio.

They are then transmitted via a VHF-FM radio link to facsimile recorders on board the ships and in shipping company offices. This process allows the ships and shipping companies to obtain a map of the thickness, type, location and extent of ice in the entire lake within one hour after the aircraft over-flight. With this map, shipping companies can dispatch ships with safe assurance and ship captains can plot safe and efficient courses.

This system was made operational during the 1974-75 winter season and enabled ships to navigate the Great Lakes without interruption through the entire winter season.

The Philip R. Clark *dressed up for Christmas with colored lights in the after section.*

The Christmas menu for U.S. Steel sailors who are aboard ship during Christmas.

Christmas Aboard a Vessel

There are obvious hardships in sailing during the winter months but perhaps none strike the Great Lakes seaman quite so hard as spending Christmas Day aboard a carrier in transit through ice. The owners of the ships, as well as the men who run them, work hard to make the situation as pleasant as possible.

Last year, for instance, on December 25th, a silver-stacked vessel of the U.S. Steel fleet moved out of Lake Superior toward Whitefish Bay and the Soo Locks. From the south, another U.S. Steel vessel edged its way through heavy snow in the St. Marys River. Obviously Christmas could be better.

"It's not the usual kind of Christmas," notes one crew member. "You don't have the bustle, the crowds, the noise or all the lights, but you do find a special meaning in the sound of a quiet night—a sense of awe and expectation, that carries for us all, a Christmas message."

"You miss your family naturally," says another. "Yet, many crews who have been sailing together for a season have a special sense of unity that's the next best thing to a family. And you're especially aware of it at Christmas time."

Before the efforts to operate throughout the winter in the Great Lakes, most vessels did not normally operate as late as Christmas Day. Winter traditionally closed the season in early December, and crews of the Great Lakes fleet were usually home for the holidays.

Things are different now.

But from the bridge of the crew quarters on a long boat, you can find a warmth and a sense of good will that compensates for the cold winds and black, winter waters. Christmas trees, Santa Clauses and garlands brighten the ship. From the galley comes a promise of an exciting Christmas dinner. There are no duty assignments for the day, only those needed to keep the vessel operating must work. A special menu is planned by the chief steward, and dinner is served in a decorated galley. A typical menu is shown elsewhere on this page.

Crewmen get into the act too, with festive outside decorations carrying greetings from the crew to the people on the land the vessel passes as it moves through the St. Marys River or the Mackinac Straits.

A calm afternoon near the Massena locks.

11

What Happens Next?

There are three broad areas of change that can affect the future of the Great Lakes fleet, other than, of course, the achievement of a longer shipping season and the concomitant change this fact would bring to vessel design and to regional economies. These broad areas are changes in cargo movement, in port facilities and in vessel characteristics. The former is spelled out quite graphically in a 1976 study funded by the University of Wisconsin's Sea Grant Program. Dr. Eric Schenker, Harold M. Mayer and Harry C. Brockel, all from the Center for Great Lakes Studies at that University, point to shifts in cargo movement as a historically re-occuring fact of life in the Great Lakes.

"The internal Great Lakes transportation system is unique in its specialization," the study indicates, "and in its adaption to regional resources."

"Three dominant commodities, iron ore, coal and limestone are strategically located around the Lakes. They provide the genesis for the western hemisphere's largest concentration of iron and steel manufacturing and for other industries dependent on iron and steel. The hinterland, both in Canada and the United States, embraces some of the most productive grain lands in the world; important centers of food processing and grain mil-

ling and areas of dairy production and meat packing.

"The Lake transportation system early tailored itself to move these resources and, in so doing, the automation of bulk cargo handling occurred. The self-unloading ship, considered a triumph of modern technology, appeared on the Great Lakes ... climaxing with a new fleet of 1,000 ft. self-unloading vessels. Automation was developed on shore equally early with the Hulett unloaders, giant cranes and shore-side conveyor systems for bulk cargo."

"Traders in the Seaway bulk cargo system like to remind their more worldly colleagues that what is new on the oceans is two generations old on the Lakes, the authorities note...

"The large Lake bulk freighter, operated within the confines of the five Great Lakes, adapted itself to the new opportunities of the St. Lawrence Seaway, and with great flexibility engaged in the transport of grain from the western Great Lakes to St. Lawrence River elevators, and the new westerly movement of iron ore from Quebec-Labrador back into the Great Lakes. *In effect, the traditional pattern of iron ore from west to east, was partially reversed, and an important new movement of iron ore developed from east to west, with grain, coal and stone balancing out the vessel movements ...*" (italics ours)

A very cold day at sea.

"With the decline of open pit iron mining in the Mesabi and other Lake Superior ranges, and with cost inflation justifying new ventures, taconite has emerged in the Great Lakes region as a major commodity, while direct-shipping iron ore production has shifted from the western Great Lakes region to eastern Canada."

Then too, the authors point out, "Within the Great Lakes, shipping technology is responding to shifts of resources and industrial method. With the advent of the energy crisis, the movement of coal has increased dramatically in the past few years."

Schenker *et. al.* also point to the fact that as cargoes are shifted, so will port characteristics change—with the growth of some ports and, of course, the diminishing (or even the disappearance) of others.

Ports, they note, as presently constituted in the Lakes region, must adequately respond to shifting traffic, to new shipping technologies, to inflationary pressures . . . and to a considerable atmosphere of uncontrolled change.

Changes in vessel technology are also subject to rapid change, in fact, changes are occurring so rapidly in the Great Lakes that it is hard to keep abreast of them. For instance, the Corps of Engineers has recently recommended that still larger ore carriers—larger than the new super-lakers be permitted to transit Saulte Ste. Marie, opening the way for even greater ore fleets. They are talking 1,100 ft. vessels.

Responding to a request from the Lake Carriers' Association to analyze the safety, engineering, economic and environmental effects of 1100′ x 105′ vessels on the Poe Lock at

The U.S. Steel fleet dressed up for the Bicentennial. Here, the Arthur M. Anderson *and the* Cason J. Calloway *show bright and colorful bow colors in celebration of the nation's 200th birthday.*

Sault Ste. Marie, connecting channels and servicing harbors, the Corps' special report said that vessels plying the Lakes could, in actuality, be 100 feet longer than the 1,000 x 105 ft. super-lakers.

According to the Corps, an estimated annual transportation savings of almost $4 million would result from the additional 100 feet in vessel length. Transportation and energy savings would develop from larger ships making less trips, and at a lower cost per ton. Tonnage capacity of the Poe would increase and so would the efficiency of the existing upper Great Lakes System.

Lockage demonstrations were held at Sault Ste. Marie during the summer of 1976 to observe a simulated transit of 1100 ft. vessels. They showed the proposed transiting procedures to be practical.[16]

Traditional methods of navigation in connecting channels, particularly in critical bends of the St. Marys River, would be altered by the 1,100 ft. super-laker. Navigation aids applied now to the super-lakers would also work for the 1,100 ft. ships, including the trend toward greater maneuverability with twin screws, twin rudders and bow and stern thrusters.

Would harbors and docks be able to service 1,100 foot super-lakers? Some would. These include: (loading) Duluth, Superior, Two Harbors, Silver Bay, Taconite Harbor, Marquette, Escanaba and (unloading) Chicago, Burns Harbor, Gary, Detroit, Toledo and, with slight modification, Lorain.

[16]Transit time of the 1,100 ft. freighter is estimated to be 10 minutes longer than that of the existing super-laker.

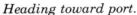

Heading toward port.

The Lake Carriers' Association strongly favored a regulation change to allow 1,100 ft. lake carriers to transit the Soo, but expresses concern that today only the Poe Lock is equipped to handle the larger vessels; they urge construction of a second, larger lock.

So we see the emerging trend: The rapidly increasing needs of the nation for the resources of the Great Lakes region coupled with the necessarily expanding facilities to convert the resources into useable commodities.

And functioning between mine and mill, grain elevator and factory, quarry and industrial complex, coal field and electrical generating plant, is the lake carrier. As the needs of the nation change so will the configuration of the fleet. The advent of Federal subsidies and, even more so, of Title XI loan guarantees in the Lakes assure financing necessary to meet the demands of an expanding nation.

More carriers? More certainly—larger ones, too. And as the probability of an extended winter navigation season finds its way into the future of the fleet, we will look for the retirement of older vessels in favor of newer, ice-strengthened ore boats which can transit the ice fields and the furrows of the Great Lakes in winter.

Larger, stronger vessels.

But hasn't that always been the story? From the bateau to the barquentine, from the schooner to the whaleback, from the *Onoko*-class carrier to the *Cort* and the *Presque Isle* and the *Barker*, the lake carrier has historically moved in the precise direction of increased size and strength. And so, it seems, the future for the lake carrier is an extension of the past. And it is obviously a future as dramatic as the change from sail to steam, from wood to iron and steel.

The fresh water merchant marine of the United States and Canada—combined, one of the largest, most potent maritime fleets in the world—will get bigger, will get better, in the decades ahead. It must. Two nations require it, depend upon it, even demand it. The lake carrier will respond to the requirement, the dependency, the demand. And its story will go on from there.

THE END

A view from the bridge.

A vessel approaches a lake marker.

The Wagner *sits along the lock wall while the Papachristidis Company's 730-ft. vessel the* Grand Herminie *moves out of the lock at low water. The* girders in the foreground belong to Seaway gate lifting equipment which stands by at all times in case of damage to the lock gates.

APPENDIX: THE FLEET

The vessels that comprise the fleet of the Great Lakes broadly divide into three categories. The larger members—some 145 vessels — belong to the U.S. Lake Carriers' Association, 149 are affiliated with the Canadian Dominion Marine Association and the rest — no one has ever counted all of these, if you include tugs, barges, work boats and the like — belong to neither organization.*

To view the Great Lakes fleet as it exists today, it is important to develop an overview of the structure of these two organizations, which we dealt with in the early pages of this volume. The Lake Carriers' Association as we have seen, consists of 15 member companies, controlling 145 vessels with a total gross registered tonnage of 1.5 million, and a carrying capacity of 2.6 million tons.

A summary of the Lake Carriers' Association membership looks like this:

*Although every attempt has been made to identify the ships of the U.S. and Canadian Great Lakes fleets, some few vessels for one of a number of reasons may not be listed. Such an omission does not signify an oversight, but rather the unavailability of documented information.

	No. Of Vessels	Total Gross Reg. Tonnage	Carrying Capacity Gross Tons
Bethlehem Steel Corporation	6	85,018	165,300
Boland & Cornelius, Inc., Managers	18	198,413	325,900
Cleveland-Cliffs Iron Co.	14	131,071	232,135
Cleveland Tankers, Incorporated	4	14,740	18,468
Erie Sand Steamship Company	3	12,856	16,550
Ford Motor Company	5	50,263	84,900
Hanna Mining Company, Agents	7	79,850	149,000
Huron Cement Division	6	31,275	50,400
Inland Steel Company	6	56,505	100,500
The Interlake Steamship Company	11	119,630	220,950
International Harvester Company	1	7,984	13,600
Litton Great Lakes Corporation	1	24,199	52,000
Medusa Cement Company	2	12,906	22,000
Oglebay Norton Company - Columbia Transportation Div.	17	168,808	297,000
United States Steel Corporation	44	398,562	705,776
	145	1,392,080	2,454,479

ALPHABETICAL LIST OF VESSELS IN LAKE CARRIERS' ASSOCIATION WITH NAMES OF OWNERS OR MANAGERS

A

Vessel	Owner or Manager
Affleck, B.F.	U.S. Steel Corp.
Anderson, A.M.	U.S. Steel Corp.
Armco	Oglebay Norton Co.
Ashland	Oglebay Norton Co.
Avery, Sewell	U.S. Steel Corp.
Ayers, J. Burton	Oglebay Norton Co.

B

Barker, James R.	Interlake Steamship Co.
Beeghly, Chas. M.	Interlake Steamship Co.
*Block, E.J.	Inland Steel Co.
Block, L.E.	Inland Steel Co.
Block, Philip D.	Inland Steel Co.
Blough, Roger	U.S. Steel Corp.
Boland, John J.	Boland & Cornelius
Boyer, W.B.	Cleveland-Cliffs Iron Co.

Oglebay Norton's 715-ft. carrier **Middletown**.

Vessel	Owner or Manager
Breech, E.R.	Ford Motor Co.
Buckeye	Oglebay Norton Co.
Buffington, E.J.	U.S. Steel Corp.
*Block, J.L.	Inland Steel Co.

C

Cadillac	Cleveland-Cliffs Iron Co.
Calcite II	U.S. Steel Corp.
Callaway, C.J.	U.S. Steel Corp.
Carnahan, P.H	The Hanna Fleet
Champlain	Cleveland-Cliffs Iron Co.
Clarke, Philip R	U.S. Steel Corp.
Clemson, D.M.	U.S. Steel Corp.
Cliffs Victory	Cleveland-Cliffs Iron Co.
Clymer, I.L.	U.S. Steel Corp.
Cole, Thomas F.	U.S. Steel Corp.
Consumers Power	Boland & Cornelius
Cornelius, Adam E.	Boland & Cornelius
Cort, S.J.	Bethlehem Steel Corp.
Coulby, Harry	Interlake Steamship Co.
Crapo, S.T.	Huron Cement Divn.

D

Detroit Edison	Boland & Cornelius
Diamond Alkali	Boland & Cornelius
Dinkey, Alva C.	U.S. Steel Corp.
Dykstra, John	Ford Motor Co.

F

Fairless, B.F.	U.S. Steel Corp.
Falk, Jr., Leon	The Hanna Fleet
Farrell, James A.	U.S. Steel Corp.
Ferbert, A.H.	U.S. Steel Corp.
Ford, Benson	Ford Motor Co.
Ford, Emory M.	Huron Cement Divn.
Ford, Henry, II	Ford Motor Co.
Ford, John B.	Huron Cement Divn.
Ford, Wm. Clay	Ford Motor Co.
Frantz, Joseph H.	Oglebay Norton Co.
Fraser, Leon	U.S. Steel Corp.
Frontenac	Cleveland-Cliffs Iron Co.

G

Girdler, Tom M.	Cleveland-Cliffs Iron Co.
Grace, E. G.	Interlake Steamship Co.
Greene, Edw. B.	Cleveland-Cliffs Iron Co.

H

Harriman, L.G.	Huron Cement Divn.
Hatfield, Joshua A.	U.S. Steel Corp.
Holloway, W.W.	Oglebay Norton Co.
Homer, A.B.	Bethlehem Steel Corp.
Hoyt 2nd, Elton	Interlake Steamship Co.
Hulst, John	U.S. Steel Corp.
Humphrey, Geo. M.	The Hanna Fleet
Hutchinson J.T.	Boland & Cornelius

I

Iglehart, J.A.W.	Huron Cement Divn.
International, The	International Harvester Co.
Irvin, Wm. A.	U.S. Steel Corp.

J

Jackson, H.C.	Interlake Steamship Co.
Johnson, Horace	U.S. Steel Corp.
Johnstown	Bethlehem Steel Corp.
Jupiter	Cleveland Tankers

K

Kerr, D.G.	U.S. Steel Corp.
Kling, John A.	Boland & Cornelius
Kyes, Roger M.	Boland & Cornelius

L

Lakewood	Erie Sand Steamship Co.
Lamont, Thomas W.	U.S. Steel Corp.
Laud, Sam	Boland & Cornelius
Lehigh	Bethlehem Steel Corp.
Lindabury, Richard V.	U.S. Steel Corp.

M

Mather, Samuel	Interlake Steamship Co.
Mather, Wm. G.	Cleveland-Cliffs Iron Co.
Mauthe, J.L.	Interlake Steamship Co.
McCullough, Jr., C.H.	Medusa Cement Co.
McGonagle, W.A.	U.S. Steel Corp.
McKee Sons	Boland & Cornelius
Medusa Challenger	Medusa Cement Co.
Middletown	Oglebay Norton Co.
Miller, Gov.	U.S. Steel Corp.
Morgan, J.P., Jr.	U.S. Steel Corp.
Munson, John G.	U.S. Steel Corp.

N

Niagara	Erie Sand Steamship Co.
Nicolet	Boland & Cornelius
Norton, R.C.	Oglebay Norton Co.

O

Oglebay, Crispin	Oglebay Norton Co.
Olds, Irving S.	U.S. Steel Corp.

P

Pargny, Eugene W.	U.S. Steel Corp.
Patton, Thos. F.	Cleveland-Cliffs Iron Co.
Polaris	Cleveland Tankers, Inc.
Pontiac	Cleveland-Cliffs Iron Co.
Presque Isle	Litton Great Lakes Corp.

R

Randall, C.B.	Inland Steel Co.
Reiss, Raymond H.	Cleveland-Cliffs Iron Co.
Reiss, Richard J.	Boland & Cornelius
Reiss, Wm. A.	Oglebay Norton Co.
Reserve	Oglebay Norton Co.
Richardson, W.C.	Oglebay Norton Co.
Robinson, T.W.	U.S. Steel Corp.
Roesch, William R.	Oglebay Norton Co.
Rogers City	U.S. Steel Corp.
Ryerson, E.L.	Inland Steel Co.

The Grand Enterprise.

Vessel	Owner or Manager
S	
St. Clair	Boland & Cornelius
Saturn	Cleveland Tankers, Inc.
Schiller, Wm. B.	U.S. Steel Corp.
Schoellkopf, Jr., J.F.	Erie Sand Steamship Co.
Sensibar, J.R.	Oglebay Norton Co.
Sharon	Boland & Cornelius
Sherwin, John	Interlake Steamship Co.
Sloan, George A.	U.S. Steel Corp.
Snyder, Jr., Wm. P.	Cleveland-Cliffs Iron Co.
Sparrows Point	Bethlehem Steel Corp.
Stanley, Robert C.	U.S. Steel Corp.
·elton	Bethlehem Steel Corp.
Sterling, W.A.	Cleveland-Cliffs Iron Co.
Sykes, Wilfred	Inland Steel Co.
Sylvania	Oglebay Norton Co.
T	
Taylor, Myron C.	U.S. Steel Corp.
Thayer, Paul	Oglebay Norton Co.
Thomas, Eugene P.	U.S. Steel Corp.
Thompson, J.H.	The Hanna Fleet
Tomlinson, G.A.	Oglebay Norton Co.
Townsend, P.H.	Huron Cement Divn.
V	
Voorhees, Enders M.	U.S. Steel Corp.
W	
Watson, Ralph H.	U.S. Steel Corp.
Weir, Ernest T.	The Hanna Fleet
West, Charles C.	Boland & Cornelius
White, Chas. M.	Cleveland-Cliffs Iron Co.
White, H. Lee	Boland & Cornelius
Williams, Homer D.	U.S. Steel Corp.
Wilson, Charles E.	Boland & Cornelius
Wilson, Thomas	Oglebay Norton Co.
Wolverine	Oglebay Norton Co.
Y	
Young, Jos. S.	Boland & Cornelius
Z	
Ziesing, August	U.S. Steel Corp.

The Dominion Marine Association serves 18 members with 149 vessels, with tonnage in excess of 2,000,000 and a capital investment of more than $500 million.

Member companies include:

Algoma Central Railway, Sault Ste. Marie, Ont. (10 vessels)

Algoma Steel Corp., Ltd., Sault Ste. Marie, Ont. (1 vessel)

Canada Cement Lafarge, Ltd., Montreal, P.Q. (1 vessel)

Canada Steamship Lines, Ltd., Montreal, P.Q. (30 vessels)

Carryore, Ltd., Westmount, P.Q. (2 vessels)

Gulf Oil Canada, Ltd., Toronto, Ont. (1 vessel)

Hall Corp. Shipping, Ltd., Montreal, P.Q. (21 vessels)

Hindman Transportation Co., Ltd., Owen Sound, Ont. (5 vessels)

Imperial Oil, Ltd., Toronto, Ont. (9 vessels)

Mohawk Navigation Co., Ltd., Montreal, P.Q. (2 vessels)

N.M. Paterson & Sons, Ltd., Thunder Bay, Ont. (16 vessels)

National Sand & Material Co., Hamilton, Ont. (1 vessel)

Quebec & Ontario Transportation Co., Ltd., St. Catharines, Ont. (6 vessels)

Scott Misener Steamships, Ltd., St. Catharines, Ont. (8 vessels)

Shell Canadian Tankers, Ltd., Toronto, Ont. (6 vessels)

Texaco Canada, Ltd., Toronto, Ont. (2 vessels)

Upper Lakes Shipping, Inc., Toronto, Ont. (22 vessels)

Westdale Shipping, Ltd., Port Credit, Ont. (6 vessels)

The John Sherwin *heads for the Ambassador Bridge in the Detroit River.*

An alphabetical listing of Great Lakes vessels in the Dominion Marine Association:

A

Vessel	Owner/Operator
Agawa Canyon	Algoma Central Railway
Algocen	Algoma Central Railway
Algorail	Algoma Central Railway
Algosoo	Algoma Central Railway
Algoway	Algoma Central Railway
Angus, R. Bruce	Upper Lakes Shipping, Ltd.
Arctic Trader	Shell Canada, Ltd.
Avondale	Westdale Shipping, Ltd.

B

Baffin Transport	Hall Corp. Shipping, Ltd.
Barber, E.B.	Algoma Central Railway
Bayshell	Shell Canada, Ltd.
Bay Transport	Hall Corp. Shipping, Ltd.
Beavercliffe Hall	Hall Corp. Shipping, Ltd.
Black Bay	Canada Steamship Lines, Ltd.
Black River	Quebec & Ontario Transp. Co., Ltd.

C

Vessel	Owner/Operator
Calgadoc	N.M. Paterson & Sons, Ltd.
Canadian Century	Upper Lakes Shipping, Ltd.
Canadian Hunter	Upper Lakes Shipping, Ltd.
Canadian Leader	Upper Lakes Shipping, Ltd.
Canadian Mariner	Upper Lakes Shipping, Ltd.
Canadian Progress	Upper Lakes Shipping, Ltd.
Canadoc	N.M. Paterson & Sons, Ltd.
Cape Breton Miner	Upper Lakes Shipping, Ltd.
Cape Transport	Hall Corp. Shipping, Ltd.
Carl, George M.	Scott Misener Steamships, Ltd.
Cementkarrier	Canada Cement LaFarge, Ltd.
Chemical Transport	Hall Corp. Shipping, Ltd.
Chicago Tribune	Quebec & Ontario Transp. Co., Ltd.
Comeaudoc	N.M. Paterson & Sons, Ltd.
Cove Transport	Hall Corp. Shipping, Ltd.

D

Dick, Charles	National Sand & Material Co., Ltd.
Doan Transport	Hall Corp. Shipping, Ltd.
Dunn, Sir James	Canada Steamship Lines, Ltd.

E

Eastern Shell	Shell Canada, Ltd.
English River	Canada Steamship Lines, Ltd.
Eskimo	Canada Steamship Lines, Ltd.
Evans, Helen	Hindman Transportation Co., Ltd.
Evans, Parker	Hindman Transportation Co., Ltd.

F

Vessel	Owner/Operator
Ferndale	Westdale Shipping, Ltd.
Fort Chambly	Canada Steamship Lines, Ltd.
Fort Henry	Canada Steamship Lines, Ltd.
Fort St. Louis	Canada Steamship Lines, Ltd.
Fort William	Canada Steamship Lines, Ltd.
Fort York	Canada Steamship Lines, Ltd.
France, John A.	Scott Misener Steamships, Ltd.
Frankcliffe Hall	Hall Corp. Shipping, Ltd.
Franqueline	Quebec & Ontario Transp. Co., Ltd.
French River	Canada Steamship Lines, Ltd.
Frobisher Transport	Hall Corp. Shipping, Ltd.
Frontenac	Canada Steamship Lines, Ltd.
Fuel Marketer	Shell Canada, Ltd.

G

Georgian Bay	Canada Steamship Lines, Ltd.
Gleneagles	Canada Steamship Lines, Ltd.
Glossbrenner, A.S.	Algoma Central Railway
Goderich	Upper Lakes Shipping, Ltd.
Golden Hind	Quebec & Ontario Transp. Co., Ltd.
Griffith, H.M.	Canada Steamship Lines, Ltd.
Gulf Canada	Gulf Oil Canada, Ltd.

American Steamship's self-unloader Consumers Power.

The self-unloader Myron C. Taylor *from U.S. Steel.*

Vessel	Owner/Operator
Senneville	Mohawk Navigation Co., Ltd.
Sherman, Frank A.	Upper Lakes Shipping, Ltd.
Silver Isle	Mohawk Navigation Co., Ltd.
Simcoe	Canada Steamship Lines, Ltd.
Stadocona	Canada Steamship Lines, Ltd.

T

Tadoussac	Canada Steamship Lines, Ltd.
Tarantau	Canada Steamship Lines, Ltd.
Texaco Brave	Texaco Canada, Ltd.
Texaco Chief	Texaco Canada, Ltd.
Thornhill	Upper Lakes Shipping, Ltd.
Troisdoc	N.M. Paterson & Sons, Ltd.

U

Vessel	Owner/Operator
Ungava Transport	Hall Corp. Shipping, Ltd.

V

Vaie St. Paul	Canada Steamship Lines, Ltd.

W

Westdale	Westdale Shipping, Ltd.
Wheat King	Upper Lakes Shipping, Ltd.

Y

Yankcanuck	Algoma Steel Corp., Ltd.

There are a number of owners/operators of Great Lakes vessels who do not belong to either the Lake Carriers' or Dominion Marine. The vessels they operate — bulkers, tankers, passenger liners, dredges, scows, barges — number in the hundreds.

Some fifty of the typical Independents are listed here, along with the vessels they normally operate, in order to give the reader a feel for this aspect of the Great Lakes maritime picture. The listing is by no means a compendium of all the independent vessels or owners on the lakes: this kind of a categorization would take virtually a book in itself, or more.

Readers wishing to explore further the backgrounds and statistical data on specific Great Lakes ships are encouraged. Contact Freshwater Press at 258, The Arcade, Cleveland, Ohio 44114 for several books on these subjects by John Greenwood, a noted Great Lakes expert, or the Great Lakes Red Book, published by the Fourth Seacoast Publishing Company of St. Clair Shores, Mich.

Allied Bunkering Service (1 vessel)
American Can of Canada, Ltd. (1 vessel)
American Steamship Co. (12 vessels)
Amersand Steamship Corp. (1 vessel)
Amoco Oil Co. (3 vessels)
Atlantic Richfield Co. (2 vessels)
Ann Arbor Railroad Co. (2 vessels)
Bigane Vessel Fueling Co., Inc. (1 vessel)
Bob-Lo Co. (2 vessels)
Branch Lines, Ltd. (10 vessels)
John H. Bultema (1 vessel)
Canadian National Railways (4 vessels)
Canadian Pacific Railway Co. (1 vessel)
Chessie System, Inc. (4 vessels)
Comet Enterprises, Ltd. (2 vessels)
Construction Aggregates Corp. (1 vessel)
Eder Barge & Towing, Inc. (1 vessel)
Equipment House, Ltd. (1 vessel)
Erie Navigation Co. (3 vessels)
Erie Sand & Gravel Co., Esco Dredge & Fill Div. (1 vessel)
Harry Gamble Shipyards (1 vessel)

Gartland Steamship Co. (2 vessels)
Grand Trunk-Milwaukee Car Ferry Co. (3 vessels)
Gulf Oil Corp. (1 vessel)
Hansand Steamship Corp. (1 vessel)
Incan Ships, Ltd. (1 vessel)
Johnstone Shipping, Ltd. (2 vessels)
Kinsman Marine (13 vessels)
Lake Erie Sand and Transport Co. (1 vessel)
Liquilassie Shipping, Ltd. (1 vessel)
Loraine Elyria Sand Co. (1 vessel)
Mackinac Transportation Co. (1 vessel)
A.B. McLean & Sons, Ltd. (2 vessels)
McNamara Marine, Ltd. (1 vessel)
Marine Fueling, Inc. (3 vessels)
Michigan Tankers, Inc. (1 vessel)
National Sand and Gravel Co. (1 vessel)
National Steel Corp. (6 vessels)
Nipigon Transport, Ltd. (2 vessels)
Norfolk and Western Railway (4 vessels)
Ontario-Lake Erie Sand, Ltd. (1 vessel)
Ontario Northland Transportation Commission (3 vessels)
Oswego Barge Co. (1 vessel)
Panoceanic Engineering Corp. (1 vessel)
Penn-Dixie Cement Corp. (1 vessel)
Trico Enterprises, Ltd. (1 vessel)
Reiss Steamship Co. (3 vessels)
S & E Shipping Corp. (2 vessels)
Sand Products Corp. (1 vessel)
Selvick Marine Towing Corp. (1 vessel)
White Brothers Sand, Inc. (1 vessel)
Wisconsin and Michigan Steamship Co. (2 vessels)

An alphabetical listing of many of the larger Great Lakes vessels whose owners are not members of the Lake Carriers' Association or the Dominion Marine Association:

A

Vessel	Owner/Operator
Allen, Harry L	Kinsman Marine Transit Co.
American	Construction Aggregates Corp.
Amoco Illinois	Amoco Oil Co.
Amoco Indiana	Amoco Oil Co.
Amoco Wisconsin	Amoco Oil Co.
Aquarama	Sand Products Corp.
Atkinson, Arthur K.	Ann Arbor Railroad Co.
Austin, C.L.	Kinsman Marine Transit Co.

B

Vessel	Owner/Operator
Badger	Chessie System, Inc.
Bennett, William H.	Marine Fueling, Inc.
Bigane, Joseph F.	Bigane Vessel Fueling Co., Inc.
Boland, John J.	American Steamship Co.

C

Vessel	Owner/Operator
Cadwell, C.W.	Equipment House, Ltd.
Carnahan, Paul H.	National Steel Corp.
Cedarbranch	Branch Lines, Ltd.
Chi-Cheemaun	Ontario Northland Transp. Comm.
Chicago Trader	Kinsman Marine Transit Co.
Chief Wawatam	Mackinac Transportation Co.
City of Midland	Chessie System, Inc.
City of Milwaukee	Grand Trunk-Milwaukee Car Ferry Co.
Columbia	Bob-Lo Co.
Congar	Johnstone Shipping, Ltd.
Consumers Power	American Steamship Co.
Cornelius, Adam E.	American Steamship Co.

D

Vessel	Owner/Operator
Denton	Kinsman Marine Transit Co.
Detroit	Michigan Tankers, Inc.
Detroit	Norfolk & Western Railway
Detroit Edison	American Steamship Co.
Diamond Alkali	American Steamship Co.

E

Vessel	Owner/Operator
Edington, W.M.	Ontario-Lake Erie Sand, Ltd.
Elmbranch	Branch Lines, Ltd.
Emery, John R.	Erie Navigation Co.
Erie	Lake Erie Sand & Transport Co.
Everest, D.C.	American Can of Canada, Ltd.

F

Vessel	Owner/Operator
Falk, Leon, Jr.	National Steel Corp.

The Arsene Simard, *a Branch Lines Tanker.*

G

Gary	Atlantic Richfield Co.
Goble, George D.	Kinsman Marine Transit Co.
Grand Rapids	Grand Trunk-Milwaukee Car Ferry Co.
Great Lakes	Atlantic Richfield Co.

H

Hennepin	Gartland Steamship Co.
Heron Bay	Comet Enterprises, Ltd.
Highway 16	Wisconsin & Michigan Steamship Co.
Holst, R.W.	White Brothers Sand, Inc.
Humphrey, George M.	National Steel Corp.
Huntley, Charles R.	McNamara Marine, Ltd.
Huron	Canadian National Railways
Husky 120	Garry Gamble Shipyards
Hutchinson, John T.	American Steamship Co.

I

| Incan Superior | Incan Ships, Ltd. |

J

| Johnson, Charles W. | A.B. McLean & Sons, Ltd. |

K

Kinsman Enterprise	Kinsman Marine Transit Co.
Kling, John A.	Reiss Steamship Co.
Kyes, Roger M.	American Steamship Co.

L

LaDuca, L.G. II	Allied Bunkering Service
Lake Manitoba	Nipigon Transport, Ltd.
Lake Winnipeg	Nipigon Transport, Ltd.
Lansdowne	Canadian National Railways
Lawson, A.T.	S. & E. Shipping Corp.
Lesco	Lorain Elyria Sand Co.
Lil' Rock	Erie Sand & Gravel Co.
Liquilassie	Liquilassie Shipping, Ltd.
Lyons, James B.	National Sand & Gravel Co.

M

Vessel	Owner/Operator
McCurdy, Merle M.	Kinsman Marine Transit Co.
McKee Sons	Amersand Steamship Corp.
Madison	Grand Trunk-Milwaukee Car Ferry Co.
Maitland No. 1	Eder Barge & Towing, Inc.
Malden	A.B. McLean & Sons, Ltd.
Manistee	John H. Bultema
Manitowoc	Norfolk & Western Railway
Manske, Fred A.	American Steamship Co.
Maplebranch	Branch Lines, Ltd.
Marine Fuel II	Marine Fueling, Inc.
Marine Fuel Oil	Marine Fueling, Inc.
Massey D.	Panoceanic Engineering Corp.
Millsop, Thomas E.	National Steel Corp.
Milwaukee Clipper	Wisconsin & Michigan Steamship Co.
Moreell, Ben	S. & E. Shipping Corp.

N

National Trader	National Steel Corp.
Nepco 140	Oswego Barge Co.
Nicolet	Gartland Steamship Co.
Norisle	Ontario Northland Transp. Comm.
Norgoma	Ontario Northland Transp. Comm.

Lakers pass on the Seaway.

C & O Car Ferries.

The Coast Guard in the Great Lakes

The guardian of the Great Lakes is the U.S. Coast Guard, specifically the Ninth District, which has operational responsibility for the inland seas.

The Coast Guard maintains 39 stations in the Great Lakes, along with aircraft and light stations. These include the following:

Light Stations:

Michigan: Eagle Harbor, North Manitou Shoal (Leland), Lansing Shoal (Charlevoix), Rock of Ages (Hancock), Detroit, Minneapolis Shoal (Escanaba), Manitou Island (Hancock,) St. Martin Island (Escanaba), Passage Island (Hancock), Grays Reef (St. Ignace), White Shoal (St. Ignace), Point Betsie (Frankfort), Thunder Bay Island (Alpena).

Wisconsin: Devils Island (Bayfield), Sherwood Point (Sturgeon Bay), Rawley Point (Two Rivers), Green Bay, Tibbets Point (Cape Vincent).

Minnesota: Two Harbors.

Floating Units:

Vessels in the Great Lakes under Coast Guard ownership include: *Acacia, Buckthorn,* Icebreaker *Mackinaw, Ojibwa, Raritan, Pt. Steele, Woodrush,* Icebreaker *Westwind, Arundel, Kaw, Mariposa, Naughtuck* and *Sundew.* (All vessels as Coast Guard cutters with the exception of the *Westwind* and the *Mackinaw* which are icebreakers.)

Stations:

Coast Guard stations in the Great Lakes are located at:

Michigan: Detroit, Frankfort, Grand Marais, Holland, Manistee, Grand Haven, Harbor Beach, Charlevoix, Ludington, Marquette, Muskegon, Port Huron, Bay City, St. Clair Shores, St. Joseph, St. Clair Flats, Harsens Island, St. Ignace, EastTawas.

New York: Alexandria Bay, Rochester, Youngstown, Oswego. *Illinois:* Chicago, Wilmette. *Ohio:* Cleveland, Lorain, Ashtabula, Grand River, Marblehead, Toledo. *Pennsylvania:* Erie. *Minnesota:* Duluth. *Indiana:* Michigan City.

Wisconsin: Kenosha, Milwaukee, Washington Island, Cheboygan, Two Rivers, Sturgeon Bay.

Deep in the water, the 620-ft. R. Bruce Angus.

PHOTO CREDITS

Note: Photo credits are shown below in terms of the author's source for the photograph, rather than a specific photographer who might have taken it, except where the photographer is known and specifically named.

Stuart Abbey 8, 32, 72, 73 (top), 84-85, 88, 93, 97-99, 101, 104-105, 109, 112-114 (top), 116, 118 (top left and bottom right), 119-120 (right), 122 (bottom left), 123 (top left and bottom), 124-127, 130, 132 (bottom), 141 (top), 142, 153, 156, 159, 161-165, 167 (bottom), 170-172, 174-175 ★ Arctic Engineers and Constructors 167 (top) ★ Port of Chicago 36 ★ Jon Choate, inside rear flap ★ Cleveland-Cliffs Iron Co. 129 ★ Coast Guard 76, 68, 83, 166 ★ U.S. Army Corps of Engineers 94, 158 ★ Detroit Historical Society 15 ★ Detroit Marine Terminals 122 (top) ★ Dominion Marine Association 148 (bottom) ★ Seaway Port Authority of Duluth 52 ★ Great Lakes Commission 92, 148 (top) ★ Great Lakes Historical Society 90 ★ State of Indiana 123 (center) ★ Inland Steel Co. 136 ★ Lake Carriers' Association 10-11, 13-14, 23, 26-27, 34-35, 43-49, 51, 54, 64, 68-69, 73 (bottom), 77, 81-82, 87 ★ Lakehead Harbour Commission 118 (center) ★ State of Michigan 70 ★ Port of Milwaukee 17, 24, 31 ★ National Aeronautics and Space Administration (NASA) 168 ★ Niagara Frontier Transportation Authority 30, 65 ★ Oglebay-Norton Co. 74 ★ Pickands Mather & Co. 134-135, 137 (bottom right), 138-139 (bottom) ★ Pittsburgh Dock Co. 37 ★ St. Lawrence Seaway Authority 106-107 ★ St. Lawrence Seaway Development Corporation 91, 100, 102-103, 107-108, 111, 121, 140, 144, 145, 176 ★ Jack Talbot 160 (bottom) ★ Port of Toronto 66 ★ Department of Transportation 147, 150, 160 ★ U.S. Steel 169 ★ Howard Weiss 1, 19-22, 39-42, 59-62, 79-80, 114 (bottom), 117-118 (top right and bottom left), 120 (left), 122 (bottom right), 123 (top right), 132 (top), 137 (top), 139 (top), 141 (bottom), 149, 154, 173, dust jacket front.

INDEX OF SHIPS

Note: Ships are listed below alphabetically in the form of proper nouns. For example, you will find the *James R. Barker* listed under "B" and the *North America* under "N." The former will be listed as "James R. Barker," *not* as Barker, James R.